P9-CFJ-901

The Jossey-Bass Nonprofit & Public Management Series also includes:

Team-Based Fundraising
Step by Step

Team-Based Fundraising Step by Step

A Practical Guide to
Improving Results
Through Teamwork

Mim Carlson

with Cheryl Clarke

Jossey-Bass Publishers • San Francisco

The numbered list in Chapter Three, on pp. 22–23, is from *Teamwork from Start to Finish* by Fran Rees. Copyright © 1997 by Jossey-Bass Publishers. Reprinted by permission of the publisher.

The numbered list in Chapter Five, on pp. 38–39, is from *Visionary Leadership* by Bert Nanus. Copyright © 1992 by Jossey-Bass Publishers. Reprinted by permission of the publisher.

Jossey-Bass books and products are available through most bookstores. To contact Jossey-Bass directly, call (888) 378–2537, fax to (800) 605–2665, or visit our website at www.josseybass.com.

Substantial discounts on bulk quantities of Jossey-Bass books are available to corporations, professional associations, and other organizations. For details and discount information, contact the special sales department at Jossey-Bass.

Manufactured in the United States of America.

Library of Congress Cataloging-in-Publication Data

Carlson, Mim, date.
    Team-based fundraising step by step: a practical guide to improving results through teamwork/Mim Carlson, with Cheryl Clarke.— 1st ed.
        p. cm — (Jossey-Bass nonprofit & public managment series)
    Includes bibliographical references and index.
    ISBN 0-7879-4367-3 (alk. paper)
    1. Fund raising—Team work. 2. Nonprofit organizations—Finance. I. Clarke, Cheryl, date II. Title. III. Jossey-Bass nonprofit and public management series.

HV41.2 .C376 2000
658.15′224—dc21   99-059677

PB Printing   10 9 8 7 6 5 4 3 2 1   FIRST EDITION

The Jossey-Bass
Nonprofit & Public Management Series

Contents

List of Worksheets

Preface

THE YEARS AHEAD will bring new and exciting challenges for nonprofits in the area of fundraising. Wise nonprofits are already studying trends in fund development and revising how they manage their fundraising efforts.

These nonprofits are choosing a team approach as their strategy for fundraising management. This means that the board of directors, the executive director, development director (when this position exists), all other staff, and nonboard volunteers are working together strategically to raise needed dollars for their organization.

My premise is that nonprofits must adopt a team approach in fundraising to compete for the financial resources needed to sustain and expand programs. With the continually increasing growth of the nonprofit sector and continued limited resources, it makes sense that an organization, if it is going to thrive in the years ahead, will require a team to cultivate donors and bring in the funds.

The current literature on fundraising often includes a description of the advantages of using a team approach to fundraising. For instance, numerous "how to" books on fundraising contain excellent tips on getting the board involved and making sure the board chair and executive director are active fundraisers. Yet they provide only minor focus on the steps to creating an interactive board–staff–volunteer fundraising team and to managing it effectively.

Team-Based Fundraising Step by Step fills this gap in the current literature with its focus on a step-by-step approach to building a fundraising team consisting of everyone in the nonprofit. It brings together knowledge of organizational development and fundraising and shows how to move nonprofits through a team-building process to strengthen fund development.

This book will be especially useful for staff in small to medium-sized nonprofits, particularly for executive directors, development directors, or any other staff people with the task of coordinating fundraising efforts. These individuals can easily use the step-by-step approach to guide them in developing their fundraising team and getting everyone involved.

Larger nonprofits will also find the team approach helpful. These nonprofits can use the step-by-step approach to focus on a particular fundraising strategy, such as a major special event or donor campaign.

This book will be equally useful for board members of all nonprofits. They can use the step-by-step approach to become more involved in fundraising and to identify ways to interact with staff and nonboard volunteers in carrying out their responsibilities.

The book is written for the novice fundraiser who is learning the techniques of raising funds and is looking for a strategic way to involve everyone in the organization. It is also written for the seasoned professional who has years of fundraising experience and already sees the value of building a fundraising team in a nonprofit. Consultants to nonprofits will, no doubt, find these team-building ideas to be practical tools for helping their clients become more effective fundraisers.

Generally speaking, groups that commit to the ideas of this book will need to plan on a year of team building and transformation to move through the steps successfully. I provide more specific time frames throughout the book that give a sense of how long it takes to complete each step.

The step-by-step approach to building a fundraising team looks like this.

Organizing the Team

Step One: Agreeing on a team approach

Step Two: Forming the leadership group

Step Three: Building the fundraising team

Preparing the Team

Step Four: Focusing the team with a vision and mandate

Step Five: Developing the fundraising plan (goals and objectives)

Step Six: Training the team to fundraise

Taking Action (All these steps usually occur simultaneously.)

Step Seven: Identifying potential donors

Step Eight: Cultivating donors

Step Nine: Asking for contributions

Step Ten: Recognizing donors

Evaluating Progress

Step Eleven: Evaluating team progress and health

The book begins with examples of the current processes in fundraising management that are used in most nonprofits and shows why they are not working well. I compare these processes with the team approach and offer the team approach as a solution to making fundraising more effective in your organization.

Part One describes the steps necessary to build your fundraising team, starting with agreeing that a team approach is necessary and following through to building the team. Part Two brings the team into focus with a vision, mandate, and plan of action. It also describes a process to train your team effectively to fundraise. Part Three contains the steps for putting the team into action. It discusses the major tasks of fundraising: identifying prospective donors, cultivating them, asking for contributions, and recognizing their generosity. This section presents a picture of who does what on the team. To demonstrate how this approach can be applied in a nonprofit, it gives examples of organizations that are using a team approach. Part Four concludes discussion of the step-by-step approach with strategies to evaluate fundraising success as a team.

My goal in writing this book is to provide you with a clear guide to building a powerful fundraising team. I passionately believe that fundraising is most powerful when everyone in an organization participates. I ask you to participate in the dream of a nonprofit sector that successfully raises resources sufficient to meet the demands of our society. I believe that you will realize this dream more quickly by taking the time to develop a team approach to fundraising.

January 2000

Mim Carlson
Kensington, California

Acknowledgments

THIS BOOK BEGAN as a collaboration between Cheryl Clarke and myself. In fact, it was Cheryl's vision that moved us from talking about a book on a team approach to fundraising to actually writing something down. Along the way, Cheryl decided she was not able to continue as a full collaborator and became a contributing author instead. However, everyone reading this book needs to be aware of the important time and effort Cheryl spent in making the book a reality. Much of the implementation section is Cheryl's. I have made only a few modifications here and there and added worksheets. Cheryl's extensive knowledge of fundraising is apparent throughout all the chapters. Our discussions about what should be said to help organizations set up fundraising teams were invaluable to me.

Many other people helped in writing this book, and I am grateful to all of them as well. First and foremost are the many groups Cheryl and I have worked with over the years who listened to the wisdom of having a fundraising team and put our ideas into practice. These nonprofits were, and are, the testing ground and witnesses to the success of the process discussed in this book.

I also want to thank my colleagues and the training staff at the Support Center for Nonprofit Management/NDC in San Francisco. The folks at the Support Center gave many great ideas to include in this book, particularly in the area of teamwork and board development.

Equally important, I want to thank our editor Dorothy Hearst at Jossey-Bass Inc., Publishers, who patiently moved this manuscript forward to completion and calmly helped throughout the change away from a collaboration.

I am also indebted to Judi MacMurray, who worked with me from beginning to end as manuscript editor and designer extraordinaire.

Both Cheryl and I greatly appreciate the early manuscript review by Cindy Rasicot, a consultant colleague, who gave us focus and perspective. And I greatly value the thorough review of a later manuscript version by Diane Brown from the Nonprofit Assistance Group in Sebastopol, California. Diane was an immense help in shaping the book you see today.

The Authors

The Lead Author

MIM CARLSON, M.B.A., has more than twenty years of experience in the nonprofit sector and has served in staff leadership positions for most of her career. Her areas of expertise include organizational development, strategic planning, and executive transitions. Mim is a contract consultant with the Support Center for Nonprofit Management/NDC in San Francisco, and she operates her own consulting practice. She authored *Winning Grants: Step by Step* and assisted with the development and editing of John Carver's *CarverGuide* series. Mim is also adjunct faculty at Sonoma State University, where she teaches a master's level course on strategic and long-range planning. In addition, she teaches a grantsmanship course at the University of San Francisco.

Contributing Author

CHERYL CLARKE, J.D., is a fundraising consultant with more than ten years of experience in the nonprofit sector. She has served in senior development positions at the University of San Francisco and the University of California–San Francisco. Prior to transitioning to a career in fundraising, Cheryl practiced law in the areas of corporate and business transactions. Today she advises nonprofit organizations regarding annual giving programs, grantwriting, and capital campaigns. In addition to operating her own consulting practice, Cheryl is an affiliate consultant and trainer with the Support Center for Nonprofit Management/NDC in San Francisco. She has served on several boards of directors for both for-profit and non-profit corporations. Cheryl is also an award-winning writer of short stories.

Team-Based Fundraising
Step by Step

Part One

Creating the Fundraising Team

Chapter 1

Why a Team Approach Is Needed

ONE OF THE PRIMARY REASONS I am so passionate about using a team approach to raising funds is because I have experienced the lonely challenge of being the identified fundraiser for a nonprofit and feeling the heavy burden of responsibility for bringing in donor dollars, single-handedly. By contrast, I have also experienced the remarkable benefits of a team approach to fundraising and see the opportunity for organizations to use their human resources much more effectively to generate greater financial resources.

In this chapter I define the fundraising process that will be revisited throughout the book as the team is formed and taking action. The three traditional strategies used today for fundraising management in nonprofits are described, and I explain why these will no longer work in the years ahead. I then make the case for the team approach to fundraising and explain my vision of fully engaging the board of directors, staff, and non-board volunteers in the tasks of raising needed income for an organization.

Fundraising Overview

To many folks, the terms *fundraising* and *asking* are synonymous. In reality, asking is only one step, albeit a mighty important one, in a larger fundraising process that looks like this:

1. Identifying potential donors

2. Getting their attention and involvement through education and cultivation

3. Asking for a gift

4. Acknowledging their generosity and stewarding them for their next donation

As you can see, asking is actually only one step out of a four-step process of fundraising. With a team-based approach, everyone on an agency's fundraising team—board members, nonboard volunteers, and staff members—can, and should, participate in one or more of these steps and thereby be involved in the fundraising process. My experience confirms that such active participation will ensure fundraising success.

Although the four-step fundraising process is linear, activity generally occurs in all four areas at the same time within an organization. New prospects will be identified while some prospects are being cultivated. Other prospects will be solicited while donors will be recognized for their contributions. To be effective, fundraising must go on all year in all four of these areas. In most organizations, fundraising is a big job that is simply too much for one person to do, as the following three scenarios illustrate.

The Lonely Development Director Scenario

Nonprofits commonly make the decision to hire a development director (or equivalent title) to lead an organization to financial health. Although this strategy has had a reasonable track record in the past and is not necessarily a bad one, the ever-increasing competition for funds today requires organizations to use a variety of skill sets that are rarely integrated in one individual. Consequently, hiring someone to do fundraising to end financial problems and get others "off the fundraising hook" more and more frequently leads to more than disappointing results. Bringing in a development director to "save" an organization financially is unfair to the person hired and is a poor use of the nonprofit's resources.

The Over-Worked Executive Director Scenario

Sometimes the board of directors appoints the executive director to be responsible for fundraising—in addition to all the other daily activities that the executive director must accomplish. The pressure of being "the fundraiser" is exacerbated when organizations are in periods of change and growth.

In the book *Executive Leadership in Nonprofit Organizations* (Jossey-Bass, 1991), Robert Herman and Richard Heimovic point out that executive directors face two major challenges daily. One challenge is finding financial resources via a multiple set of strategies and skill sets designed to acquire sufficient funding for their nonprofit. But Herman and Heimovic point out that it is difficult for an executive director to have all the skill sets needed for taking a multiple strategy approach to fundraising. I would add that executive directors must not only have multiple skill sets for fundraising but also have multiple skill sets in program development, financial management, staff leadership, and board development. Clearly, the executive director's job is not for the faint of heart!

My experience informs me that executive directors and board members must have clear expectations regarding fundraising responsibilities. Since expecting the executive director to do all the fundraising, in addition to all the other work of this position, is impractical, a discussion on fundraising priorities for the executive director is needed. But by limiting the fundraising scope of an organization to a few priorities, opportunities may be lost that would benefit programs and build organizational capacity.

When fundraising goals are too ambitious for the priorities and time of the executive director, boards of directors then ask the executive director to explain why the fundraising goals are not met. My consulting work often begins when something has gone awry and the executive director and board of directors are at odds over who should take the "blame" for not meeting revenue goals.

In too many cases, the tension over appropriate skill sets and unmet fundraising goals builds between boards and executive directors and often results in the loss of the executive director. This loss throws the organization into a leadership crisis of a different sort as the board now struggles with the transition from one executive director to another.

It would be so much better if boards and executive directors would work together to identify the broad range of skill sets available from board members and the executive director and then develop shared expectations of one another regarding fundraising. A strong partnership could then be built in which everyone participated together to meet revenue goals for their nonprofit.

The Fundraising Board of Directors' Scenario

Yet another fundraising strategy is to give the board of directors primary responsibility to the organization for fundraising. They are expected to cultivate, solicit, and recognize donors—and do little else.

Current theory in board development states that it is the board's responsibility to give *added value* to an organization, and one of the ways to do so is by raising funds. The emphasis, though, is that this is only *one* way to add value, meaning there are many other ways that boards must participate to help an organization become successful.

Boards do need to understand that fundraising is a responsibility of theirs, but not the *only* responsibility. Their primary responsibility is to provide the oversight and assistance that is necessary to ensure that an organization is operating efficiently and wisely.

When a board becomes so focused on fundraising that they have no time for their greater responsibility of oversight in all areas of a nonprofit, they are not fulfilling their legal and ethical duties as a board of directors. Closer public scrutiny of nonprofits is being done these days, and this scrutiny requires boards to pay attention to the workings of their nonprofits in addition to supporting the organization's fundraising efforts.

Although other scenarios for fundraising management can be found in organizations, the ones mentioned above are the most common. In each of the above scenarios, the organization fails to maximize its available human resources to raise funds. Ultimately, this failure results in unmet goals for the nonprofit and only partially met needs for a community.

The Team Approach to Fundraising

The team approach to fundraising is based on the belief that each person working in a nonprofit must be involved in raising funds in order for the organization to be successful. In addition, the task of fundraising must be integrated into all aspects of a nonprofit's operations. That is, fundraising must become part of the life of the organization. If all people working in a nonprofit see themselves as fundraisers and part of the team, the task becomes a natural part of the daily work.

Many books have been written and workshops conducted in the past several years on the importance of teamwork in solving problems and performing tasks. Many for-profit corporations, and nonprofits as well, have embraced the team concept, and some have been successful in establishing strong teams and strengthening organizational performance. Studies in these organizations have shown that teams outperform the more traditional one-person approach to problem solving and achievement. It makes sense to say, then, that using a team approach to fundraising in a nonprofit will achieve better results than relying on the skills and fortitude of one person.

What Is a Team and Why Is It So Important in Fundraising?

Let's look first at defining a team. Although I recognize the potential for each reader to have a slightly different concept of what a team is, I present this definition:

A *team* is a group of people, committed to a common purpose, who enjoy working together to accomplish goals that have a positive impact on their organization and on society.

The structure I advocate for a fundraising team is a leadership group of a few key board members, staff members, and nonboard volunteers who motivate and coordinate the work of the whole team. This leadership group guides and is part of the total organizational team that is made up of the entire organization of board members, staff members, and volunteers.

Team Factors

Much of recent team theory places a heavy emphasis on performance, and I do as well. The team needs to make a visible difference for an organization, have shared goals, and feel accountable for achieving them.

Equally, a team needs to build and sustain relationships among the team members. Being a part of a team should be fun. Members should feel supported, respected, and rewarded.

Team development theory indicates several factors that must be in place for a team to be successful. A team must have specific goals to accomplish, clarified performance roles, joint accountability, a good mix of skills and expertise, strong leadership, and good relationships among members.

Generally, team success correlates highly with the number of these factors present in the group. Here is how the factors can coalesce to ensure fundraising success. A team has

1. Clear goals to accomplish: These are the current fundraising goals for the year. They may be strictly financial or may include marketing or systems-building goals in addition to generation of revenue.

2. Clarified roles for board members, other volunteers, management staff, and other staff: In a later chapter, I describe the roles of each of these team members.

3. Celebrations among team members: Everyone has participated in the achievement; everyone participates in the celebration. Conversely, each team member is accountable for goals not met or other problems that arise.

4. A diversity of skills and experience: Diversity supports healthy dialogue and creative energy. Nowhere is this more evident than in fundraising, where success is often dependent on creative new ways of generating income, a broad range of skills to build donor relationships, and the behind-the-scenes efforts of planning, data processing, and research.

5. Leadership in fundraising: This comes from two key people—the board chairperson and the executive director. (If there is a development director on staff, this person is also key.) Ideally, these individuals constitute the base of the leadership group that also includes a few board members, staff, and nonboard volunteers.

6. Good relationships: It makes sense to have a team that works well together and has fun. There are always successes to happily acknowledge and challenges to be overcome. It takes a group of people who really enjoy one another to carry out successfully the tasks that are a necessary and daily part of fundraising.

When a team is functioning well and is highly productive, you will find all these factors working. As you begin to take the first steps in building your fundraising team, keep these factors in mind. They are keys to the team's success.

Summary

In fundraising, there are *always* more tasks than one person can do. One person cannot possibly know all the people who should be cultivated or asked for funds. Nor can one person alone manage databases, write proposals, organize events, recognize contributions, and be held solely accountable for meeting annual income goals without severely restricting the potential for an organization to meet community needs.

Far more realistic is successful fund development through several people working together as a team. Tasks are shared and everyone is committed to reaching annual goals. A group with complementary skills can reach far more people, ask for many more contributions, and move much faster than any single fundraiser—no matter how expert that one person is.

Chapter 2

Agreeing on a Team Approach

AGREEMENT ON USING A TEAM APPROACH to fundraising might be brought about in several different ways. One staff person or board member may see the value of a high-performing group who raises funds for their nonprofit and bring the idea to the staff and board for discussion. Or the development committee may explore the idea of a team approach to fundraising and make this recommendation to the board and staff. Yet another way the team approach concept may be "born" in an organization is through a financial crisis that requires everyone in a nonprofit to pull together to raise money to move out of the crisis. Some nonprofits will continue to work on building a fundraising team even after the crisis is over.

Essential to beginning a discussion of a team approach is to remember that your end result is not simply becoming a team. Instead, your end result should be the increased revenues resulting from better fundraising performance in your organization. In other words, as your nonprofit begins the process of moving to a team approach, always emphasize what this fundraising strategy will do for your organization and the clients you serve.

Your discussions on taking a team approach to fundraising should cover four key topics:

- The value of using a team over relying on one individual
- The scope of the fundraising team
- The best structure and process for the scope of work
- The challenges your organization might face in moving to a team approach

Ultimately, everyone in your organization should discuss these topics, although you will probably start off thinking about each of these on your own or with just a few people. I recommend that a small group of people interested in exploring a team approach to fundraising use the above four topics as a basis for discussion and agreement. The group can then share their ideas with everyone else in the organization to broaden and deepen the discussion and eventually bring the entire nonprofit into agreement on taking a team approach.

"Everyone" in your organization means board members, nonboard volunteers, and staff. If there are just a few staff, a small number of board members, and a handful of nonboard volunteers, you may only need one or two meetings to bring everyone to agreement that a team approach to fundraising is the right strategy. If you are in a larger organization, you will probably find the need for more meetings—one with the board of directors, and one or more with staff and nonboard volunteers.

It will generally take less time to move a smaller organization to agreement because fewer meetings are required. The average time for just this first step of the process is one to three months in a smaller organization and up to four months in larger groups that want to use a team approach for all fundraising tasks.

I provide a worksheet at the end of the chapter to facilitate group conversations about a team approach and coming to agreement on using this approach. Below I offer some ideas to help you in these discussions.

The Value of a Team Approach to Fundraising

The value of using a team approach is realized largely in three categories:

1. Teams enhance fundraising performance and personal growth in individuals. When everybody in a nonprofit sees themselves as accountable for bringing in donations, a higher level of performance is generated. Team members see themselves both as mutually accountable for the success of the group and as individually responsible for their tasks. A sense of accountability often motivates people to seek training to increase the likelihood of success, and this in turn leads to personal growth. Individuals with fundraising experience are much in demand in the nonprofit sector, so career moves may be easier with the advantage of having team experience.

The fact that individuals are working together for a common purpose also increases everyone's skills in problem solving as a group and in setting mutually acceptable goals and time lines. Getting together as a team to do fundraising means building the skills necessary to work successfully as a group.

2. Teams get results. This fact has been well documented over many years of putting teams together and watching them continually meet or exceed group goals. In fundraising, this means that your team will gener-

ate the donations needed to fulfill your nonprofit's mission in the community, particularly if you have committed leaders to help teams continue to perform at a high level well after they are initiated.

3. Teams are relatively easy to form. Once a nonprofit has agreed on using a team approach to fundraising, the steps for this process are easy to follow.

Scope of the Fundraising Team

Some organizations will decide to have the fundraising team responsible for all donation-generating tasks. The team will identify prospective donors, cultivate and communicate with them, raise funds from individual donors, foundations, corporations, and any other potential prospect, and acknowledge the gift. I use this comprehensive scope as the basis of the book.

I realize, though, that not all nonprofits will need a team to do all these fundraising tasks. Some organizations may decide that their fundraising team should have a narrower scope and focus on one or two essential tasks. One example is an organization I worked with that brought staff, board, and nonboard volunteers together to plan, implement, and evaluate the major fundraising task for the year, a special event. Although I thought that it was a bit risky to depend so much on one fundraising method, I also saw that this event continued to increase in size and revenues every year. The team developed creative new ideas for the event annually, and this creative growth made the event exciting from year to year. The group worked very well together, even as some members left and new ones came onto the team, because of the focused goal of the team and the careful matching of people's skills to their tasks. They were also well organized, owing to strong leadership from the executive director, board chair, and event chair. But perhaps most important of all, the team had a lot of fun putting on the event and basking in its success.

Deciding on the scope of the fundraising team is a personal choice for a nonprofit. There is no hard-and-fast rule that tells you what the scope of work should be. You might find it helpful to answer the following questions as you think about what scope is best for your organization.

- What are the current and anticipated fundraising activities in our organization?

- Which of these activities are doing exceptionally well without using a team approach? Which activities are not doing well?

- Do we have one person who can perform at a high level to conduct one or more of these activities?

- What are some advantages to using a team approach for any or all of the activities? (Better results, greater integration with other activities, and skills building are some advantages.)

- Are there any disadvantages to a team approach for one or more of these activities?

The Best Team Structure and Process for the Scope of Work

Since much of the rest of this book covers team structure and process, I summarize this topic only briefly here. The complete fundraising team includes the leadership group, the full board, all staff (part-time, full-time, possibly even contract personnel), and any nonboard volunteers working with programs or in administration. In the comprehensive scope of fundraising I discuss throughout the book, the leadership group oversees and coordinates the work of the team. A leadership group is essential to fundraising success. It is essentially the glue that holds the team together.

Your team process is based upon who does what within your defined scope of work. For the purposes of this book, the scope of work includes the fundamental tasks of raising funds from individuals and funders. If you are a grants-driven organization (most funds come from government, corporations, and private foundations), you will undoubtedly limit your scope to this area. The process of building the team, focusing, taking action, and evaluating success will still work for you within this narrower scope. Figure 2.1 illustrates the step-by-step process of moving to a team approach to fundraising. As the arrows on the right side of the figure show, at any point in the process you may decide you are not ready to move forward and will need to go back to a previous step.

It usually will take about twelve months for the team to move through all the steps and work well together. Meanwhile, the fundraising goes on, as do the programs and other activities of the organization.

Organizations that are in the process of developing a team approach to fundraising will generally spend several months forming the leadership group, building the team, and getting it focused with a mandate and vision. Generally, the fundraising goals and objectives are developed for the following year so that current activities are not suddenly displaced with an entirely new plan. This gives everyone time to develop the goals and objectives, decide on who will do what fundraising activities, and get some necessary training. By this time, everyone should be ready and raring to go.

FIGURE 2.1

Overview of the Step-by-Step Process

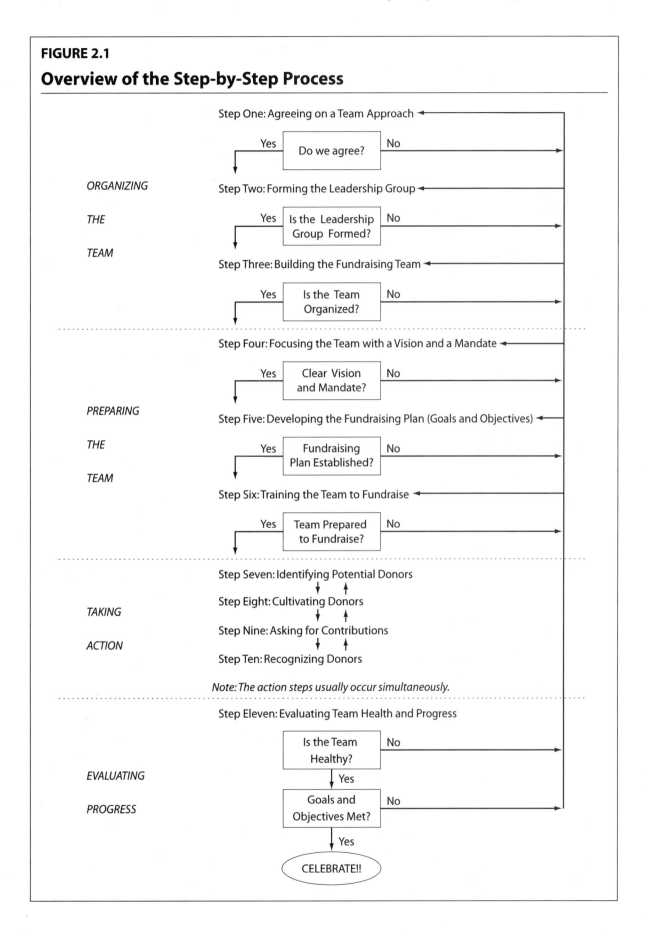

The Challenges Your Organization Might Face in Moving to a Team Approach

As you and your organization think about taking a team approach to fundraising and reflect on the scope of the team, you should also realize that you will meet challenges as you move away from your current way of fundraising toward a team approach. Your greatest challenge will very likely be resistance to letting go of the familiarity of how fundraising has always been done in your organization. A good way to manage resistance to change is to remind people that resistance is an integral part of change, and that it is normal human behavior to resist even the most beneficial of changes. Then move on to reinforcing the value of using a team approach. Highlight and emphasize the opportunity that a powerful team performance offers your nonprofit. Providing hard core resistors with a clear definition of *team* and an understanding of the team's scope of work, structure, and process will also be reassuring and helpful.

Another challenge often faced by nonprofits seeking agreement on a team approach to fundraising is the skepticism voiced by individuals who prefer to work alone rather than in groups. They may feel teams hinder the fundraising process because they get too bogged down. Or they may simply be loners who are uncomfortable with the idea of working in a group.

The best solution to this challenge is to recognize that individualism is important and that being a member of a team does not reduce that importance. What happens in a team situation is that each person's individual contribution is respected and used to build a more synergistic and creative fundraising program. In other words, people do not have to "give up" any of their individualism to be an effective team member. As the skeptics get more involved in team activities, they often get caught up in the energy created by the team.

Finally, there will always be people who do not want anything to do with fundraising. The idea of everyone being involved in this task will heighten the fear of fundraising in these individuals. One solution to this challenge is to help them build confidence by finding a fundraising task that is easy for them and is a complement to their skills. Often, some of the best fundraisers on the team express initially how fearful they are about raising money.

You may find other challenges as you move through the process of developing a fundraising team. Accept these challenges as a normal part of the process to obtaining agreement, and work together to find solutions that will allow everyone to be comfortable with the team idea. What is most important is to not ignore the fears, skepticism, and resistance you find. If you do, your next steps of forming the team, planning, and implementing the program will become more difficult to undertake.

Agreeing to a Team Approach to Fundraising— An Example

I had the opportunity to work with a regional land trust to help them agree on using a team approach to raise funds for a major land purchase and to help them form the fundraising team after the agreement was reached. The total amount needed for the land acquisition was approximately $800,000, which was quadruple the amount this group had ever raised in the eighteen-month time frame they were given by the seller.

The executive director who had primary responsibility for fundraising knew that she, alone, could not raise the $800,000. Her first step was to make sure that her board agreed on the value of acquiring this particular piece of land. Once she had affirmation of the importance of the acquisition, she pointed out the difficulty in single-handedly raising the funds.

A board meeting was dedicated to discussing the importance of a fundraising team approach for this land acquisition. We discussed the scope of work (acquiring the piece of land and funding operations), the structure (a small leadership group guiding everyone involved in some fundraising task), and the process to raise the funds (a combination of federal and state grants, major individual donors, foundations, and a media campaign).

By the time the meeting was over, everyone on the board was comfortable with the idea of a team approach to raising the $800,000. They understood that the only way they would be able to quadruple previous fundraising efforts was to have everyone involved.

This first step of agreeing to a team approach led to an incredibly successful fundraising effort. This small organization (one staff, twelve board members, a few nonboard volunteers) raised more than $800,000 in eighteen months. They are now discussing a much higher fundraising goal of raising $7 million over five years for additional land acquisitions.

Summary

Reaching agreement in your organization on taking a team approach to fundraising is your first step in building a fundraising team. To reach agreement, you will need to explore the following topics:

- The value of using a team for fundraising
- The scope of the fundraising team

- The best structure and process for the scope of work
- The challenges your organization might face in moving to a team approach

It is important to cover these topics in some detail with everyone who will be on your fundraising team. Because all board members, staff, and nonboard volunteers make up an organization's fundraising team, some teams will be quite large and others relatively small. The size of your team will generally be the major factor influencing how long it will take to reach agreement. Smaller groups may come to agreement in one meeting, whereas larger groups may require several meetings.

I recommend using Worksheet 2.1 first with a small group in your organization. After you have thoroughly explored the questions and reached agreement, use your ideas from the worksheet to help inform discussions with others in the organization. Basically, the purpose of the worksheet is to reach out and gather ideas from an ever-widening circle in your organization until everyone has had a chance to talk about the concept of a team approach to fundraising and sees some value in following this approach.

WORKSHEET 2.1

Agreeing on a Team Approach

1. What is the value of a team approach to the organization?

   •

   •

   •

   •

2. What is the work assignment for the fundraising team?

   Scope:

   Time frame:

Goals	Target Date
•	
•	
•	
•	

3. Who will make up the leadership group?

4. How will members of the fundraising team be selected?

5. How will the team ensure

   Team autonomy

   Effective communication

   Integration with other organizational activities

6. What challenges may the fundraising team meet and how can these challenges be met?

   Potential Challenges   Potential Solutions

Chapter 3
Forming the Leadership Group

ONCE YOUR ORGANIZATION has agreed to take a team approach to fundraising, your next step is to develop a leadership group. Strong leadership is the key to success for fundraising in your organization, since without this *team central* the rest of the team will flounder and may not survive. By *team central* I mean that the leadership group is at the central core as members and leaders of the whole team.

Your first task in forming a leadership group is to take a look around the organization and identify the leaders. Although there are many definitions of *leader,* in general I consider leaders as people who can successfully facilitate others to share their ideas and take action upon them. Leaders are also people who can articulate a powerful vision that inspires and motivates people.

Some leaders in your organization are easy to spot because they are at the forefront in influencing others and may already be in leadership positions. But there are also "quiet leaders" who are working hard throughout the organization, often behind the scenes, to facilitate, listen, inspire, and take action. These people could be anywhere in your nonprofit, and in any position. They are needed in your fundraising team leadership group.

Almost all nonprofits will find people within their organization who meet this description of *leader.* If you don't immediately see leadership in your group, realize that nonprofits frequently work hard to attract people with leadership skills, particularly those who will fulfill the functions of board chair and executive director. However, there are simply not enough talented leaders available for every nonprofit to enjoy instant leadership when an executive director is hired or a board chair is elected. If you believe (as I do) that leaders can be developed, it becomes essential to provide appropriate training for your key positions to give a powerful central core to your team.

Fortunately, nonprofit leadership is becoming a more recognized topic in training and seminars, so it is now easier for your organization to get help with leadership development.

Who's in Charge of the Team?

The two positions who organize and take overall responsibility for the leadership group are the board chair and the executive director. Some organizations will have different titles for these positions, and in some nonprofits, both positions may be volunteer. Below are the leadership responsibilities for each position.

The *board chairperson* sets the example for the full board in terms of performance. This person is enthusiastic about setting and achieving ambitious, yet realistic, fundraising goals. The board chairperson builds commitment among board members and makes sure that the skills and experience of board members are matched to the tasks they perform. The chairperson is also the one who must remain most conscious that fundraising is only one of the essential duties of the board of directors. Ensuring that the organization is worthy of receiving funds and that those funds are used wisely are the most essential duties of the board. The board chairperson prioritizes tasks with other team members by keeping these essential duties in mind.

The *executive director* sets the example for the rest of the staff in terms of fundraising performance. Similar to the board chairperson, the executive director is enthusiastic about goals, builds commitment among staff to raise funds, and effectively matches skills and experience to the tasks that need to be carried out. While the board chairperson is focusing on the board's performance, the executive director is focusing on the staff's performance. The executive director is also the position that manages the process of team selection and ensures the effectiveness of the team.

In some medium to larger sized nonprofits, there is often a fundraising coordinator, who may have the title of development director. If there is a fundraising coordinator, this person becomes part of the leadership group but is not a substitute or replacement for the involvement of the board chair and executive director. The executive director may, however, delegate some of the process-management functions to this position.

The development director, or fundraising coordinator, focuses primarily on implementing fundraising tasks and helps the board chair and executive director build commitment among team members. The development director is also frequently the workhorse of the team, with responsibilities for ensuring that adequate research and planning are done, finding appropriate technology, and developing written communication. Because of the coordinating role of this position, it is often the development director who organizes the leadership group meetings and takes responsibility for distribution of meeting notes describing who has agreed to do various tasks.

In the absence of a development director, your organization may have a board member who functions as a committee chair for fundraising. This person would take the same responsibilities as mentioned above for the development director.

If you are in an organization that has both a development director and a board fundraising committee chair, you are lucky indeed. Responsibilities are then generally divided between these two positions so that the board committee chair works largely with board members, and the development director works largely with staff and nonboard volunteers. Depending on the strengths of each person, either one may convene the leadership group and keep appropriate records.

Leadership Group Members

There will undoubtedly be additional members of the leadership group. You may have a key nonboard volunteer who is active in fundraising and is respected by staff and other volunteers. Some key staff may also be viewed as leaders in your organization who also understand the importance of using their skills in fundraising.

These other members can be identified by certain characteristics that are common in leaders and needed in fundraising. Members of the fundraising leadership team should be

Influential: Able to encourage others in the organization to participate; serves as a mentor and model for hesitant fundraisers

Visionary: Has a picture of what fundraising in the organization would look like if it were truly successful; is able to inspire others to hold this vision

Committed: Believes sincerely that fundraising by everyone is vitally important for success

Passionate: Holds deep feelings for the mission of the organization

Ambitious: Willing to stretch an idea or "think out of the box" in establishing a vision and setting goals; continually asks questions and probes for new ideas; takes risks

Ethical: Knows the practices of good stewardship and ensures that fundraising maintains the community's trust in the organization; engenders the trust of team members and personifies utmost integrity in all activities for the team

Articulate: Skilled in communicating the fundraising vision; demonstrates personal passion and commitment to raising funds for the organization

The board chair and executive director need to have these characteristics and should seek others in the organization who also possess them to be part of the leadership group. A development director, board fundraising committee chair, or similar position for coordinating fundraising should also have many, if not all, of the characteristics.

The executive director, board chairperson, and development director or fundraising committee chair should compare the characteristics needed for the leadership group with those of individuals in the organization with the aim of finding a small group of six to eight leaders who are willing and able to form this important group. The following worksheet is provided to help in establishing the members of the leadership group.

Worksheet 3.1 can be used to establish membership of the leadership group by individual characteristics. Individuals in the organization who are already considered leaders (board chair, executive director, development director, fundraising committee chair, for example) should first individually complete this worksheet. After everyone else under consideration for the leadership committee has completed a worksheet, these individuals should get together to discuss any gaps they see that require the recruitment of additional team members to help form the leadership group.

WORKSHEET 3.1

Leadership Characteristics

Characteristic	Personal Assessment of Strength		
	Strong	Medium	Weak
Influential: Encourages and mentors hesitant participants			
Visionary: Has a clear picture of successful fundraising			
Committed: Believes fundraising by everyone is essential			
Passionate: Dedicated to mission of organization			
Ambitious: Willing to reach for creative new ideas and take risks			
Ethical: Knows and ensures good stewardship practices			
Articulate: Skilled at communicating fundraising vision			

What to do if . . . Let's say you have a situation in which either the executive director or the board chair is not a strong fundraising leader, yet you find there is commitment in the organization among board and staff to take a team approach to fundraising. What do you do?

Proceed anyway, but with caution. This is not an ideal situation because staff and volunteers generally look to the traditional top posts in the organization to take their cues on what is important. The executive director and board chairperson must serve as members of the leadership group. However, the position can delegate some of the leadership responsibilities to others in the group. For instance, if your board chairperson is new and nervous about taking such an active role in fundraising, she or he might delegate the responsibility of building commitment for the team approach among board members and match their skills to appropriate activities. This responsibility would normally be delegated to a board fundraising committee chair, or if there is no such position, to someone on the board with a strong interest in fundraising.

Leadership Group Fundraising Skills

Once the members of a leadership group are identified, move beyond their leadership characteristics to conduct a skills inventory to ensure that the group has the necessary functional skills for fundraising. Unlike the leadership characteristics, not everyone has to have all or most of the skills listed below. You are, instead, looking for complementary skills among leadership group members, as well as missing skills to be filled by organizational team members.

The functional skills you want as part of your team are as follows (adapted from *Teamwork from Start to Finish,* by Fran Rees, published by Jossey-Bass):

1. Planning skills: You want at least one member of the leadership group who thinks strategically (takes the long view) and operationally (tracks what has to be done today). The individual(s) should also know how to develop outcome objectives and understand the key tasks that will accomplish those outcomes. A person with planning skills should also be able to coordinate other members of the leadership group and the bigger organizational team and help players determine the tasks that are most enjoyable and appropriate for them. Usually, there is a board member, staff person, or other volunteer who is an experienced planner.

2. Motivational skills: Someone on the leadership group has to move the group forward, be the cheerleader, emit continuous enthusiasm, not only with the leadership group, but also with the whole organization. Ideally, more than one person should have this role—being enthusiastic all the time can get tiring. Often, it is the executive director or board chair who has this skill.

3. Facilitative skills: The leadership group needs individuals who are able to bring the group to consensus during discussions and resolve conflicts when they emerge among group members. These facilitation skills are also needed with the whole team during meetings held on fundraising topics or when concerns about the fundraising process are raised. The people who are usually skilled facilitators are the board chairperson and the executive director.

4. Attentive to details: One leadership group member (or more) needs to pay attention to the details. This person makes sure that all the fine points are covered in terms of assignments to the leadership group and tasks agreed to by the whole group. Usually the development director has this skill.

5. Evaluative skills: One of the keys to success in teamwork is having everyone feel accountable for the actions of the group. To ensure this accountability, a person with good evaluation skills is needed on the leadership group to help put criteria in place for everyone and to help in evaluating and analyzing how the group is doing in achieving their goals. You may find a board member or staff person who is especially skilled in this area.

6. Social skills: Everyone in the leadership group should have strong social skills. These might also be called communication skills: All group members should be good listeners and good talkers. One of the joys of teamwork is being social with others, so this is a skill that is needed by all.

Worksheet 3.2 can help determine the leadership skills you need in the leadership group. To complete this worksheet, the leadership group should convene a meeting and discuss the skills listed in the worksheet. First determine the appropriate need level for your organization, then match the skill and need level to people in the leadership group.

WORSHEET 3.2 Leadership Skills		
Skills	**Level of Need (Low-Medium-High)**	**People with Skills**
Planning		• •
Motivational		• •
Facilitative		• •
Attentive to details		• •
Evaluative		• •
Social		• •

Once you have identified the leadership group based on their characteristics and skills, the group must come together and begin work. They must also begin to build trust and relationships among themselves. I will discuss in later chapters team-building exercises to help produce and reinforce these strong relationship bonds on the leadership team.

Formation of a Leadership Group—An Example

Cheryl Clarke, fundraising consultant, contributed this story of an arts education organization with which she worked that committed to using a team-based approach to fundraising. The agency was well positioned to do so as it had strong leadership from the board chair and executive director, and benefited by having capable staff support with a part-time development director.

To form the leadership group, the board chair, executive director, and development director held a couple of meetings in which they candidly reviewed the leadership characteristics and skills of the other fifteen board members. First, they identified the most committed, passionate, and influential members of the board, since they would provide the necessary leadership.

Second, they examined what specific skills each possessed. They identified one board member as a leadership group member because of her proven planning skills. Another member was selected because of his infectious enthusiasm: He would be instrumental in motivating the leadership group and the entire fundraising team. One by one, members of the leadership group were chosen. At the end of the process, which took from six to eight weeks, a leadership group comprising five board members plus the board chair, executive director, and development director had been identified.

The next step involved the board chair calling all potential members of the leadership group and inviting them to serve. In making these calls, the board chair was quick to point out what each individual brought to the leadership group, and why his or her participation was crucial. Only one board member said "no," citing that he was already overextended.

The agency's fundraising leadership group was formed and within three months they held their first meeting.

Summary

Your leadership group is the key to success in taking a team approach to fundraising because this is where commitment to this approach begins. The leadership group is part of the team, and is instrumental in forming the rest of the group and guiding it through all the steps of team development and action.

Leaders are chosen for the team based on the following characteristics: Leaders are influential, visionary, committed, passionate, ambitious, ethical, and articulate.

A good leadership group should have a variety of skills, thus providing synergistic energy to the tasks of the group. These requirements include strong planning, motivational, facilitative, attentive to detail, evaluative, and social skills.

Chapter 4

Putting Together the Rest of the Team

WHEN THE LEADERSHIP GROUP is formed, your team is beginning to take shape. Remember that the leadership group members are team members as well as leaders. The next step is to bring everyone else in the organization together as a fundraising team. Although leadership is essential to setting an example for raising funds, the other members of the team ensure a high level of performance. Whether you are identifying prospective donors, cultivating them, asking for contributions, or recognizing donor generosity, each person on the team has the responsibility to make sure that fundraising activities are carried out and goals are achieved.

Board members, staff, and nonboard volunteers often bring unique perspectives and responsibilities to the team. Even in the smallest organization, I find a variety of skills and interests among these groups. In the next section, I highlight some of the unique qualities of these groups to emphasize the importance of everyone sharing their ideas and working together.

Board of Directors' Responsibilities

The board has traditionally seen its fundraising role as a governing one. "We set policy, staff carries it out," is the phrase often heard in respect to fundraising, program development, and every other aspect of nonprofit operations. The team approach to fundraising moves beyond this line drawn in the sand that separates policy and implementation. The board sets fundraising policy along with staff and also, along with staff, ensures that those policies are implemented by meeting fundraising goals.

Upon hearing they have more than just an oversight role in fundraising, board members often state that they don't have the time, experience, contacts, or desire to carry out this function. Usually these excuses are roadblocks that can be overcome by strong team leaders who provide more reluctant members with tasks that help build their skills in raising funds. These people may be behind-the-scenes fundraisers who initially provide assistance with identifying donors, planning, writing, making improvements in technology, or cultivating donors. Or a buddy system can be developed whereby more willing board members work closely with the hesitant ones to raise funds. Sometimes a board member will be extremely reluctant to participate in fundraising but is very happy to make a large donation. (That's just fine.) All of these activities fall under the umbrella of fundraising.

It's a Duty for Board Members

The governing body of a nonprofit organization is its board of directors. As the governing body, board members have both legal responsibilities and moral ones. Among their moral duties is an obligation to the community to ensure the agency's continuing existence—at least until the societal need or problem no longer exists. A nonprofit agency will have no future unless it has enough money to pay staff salaries, rent, utilities, and to pay for programs.

Therefore, board members have an absolute obligation to make sure the agency has the financial resources to survive in the present and to thrive in the future. Most nonprofits, even those with noncontributed revenue such as fee-for-service income, need additional funds. This fact alone provides sufficient rationale for why boards must actively participate in fundraising.

What to do if . . . The reality is, though, that some board members simply will not participate in fundraising, even in behind-the-scenes tasks. Your team has no place for these individuals and it becomes the board chairperson's responsibility to ask them to leave the organization. It's important to realize that when a nonfundraising board member leaves, that person can be replaced with someone more likely to be a better team player.

Staff's Responsibilities

Staff in nonprofits also have a responsibility to raise funds. For instance, asking for a contribution and making contributions can be important roles for staff on the team.

Also, program staff members are generally the best source of information about constituents' needs, service quality, and programs that are making a difference in the community. These needs, assurances of quality, and results have to be documented and articulated to other team members for a good case to be made to prospects and donors for funds. As we all know, having a good cause is no longer enough to generate donations. Nonprofits must show results and prove that a positive impact is being made because of the high-quality programs and services of that organization. Program staff members are the key to demonstrating those positive results and thereby providing a reason for donors to give. Program staff are also good identifiers of "hot donor prospects" and can be very helpful in this important fundraising task.

Administrative staff members are often the communicators with the outside world as they answer phones, generate letters and other documents, and work overall to keep a nonprofit operating smoothly and efficiently. As a part of the team, administrative staff need to communicate to potential and current donors that their nonprofit is operating smoothly and is professionally managed. This information will instill a positive impression of the organization to donors. As in the business world, organizations that portray an image of professionalism and efficiency build confidence in the community and inspire an investment from prospective donors. Administrative staff are also able to identify potential donors through their communication, and are key cultivators of prospective donors as well as the general public. Receptionists and administrative assistants should also understand that every phone call they answer is from a current or prospective donor.

Management (in addition to the executive director and development director) join the fundraising team right alongside the staff they may supervise. Depending on their skills and interests, they may be key identifiers or cultivators of prospective donors. Managers who have strong writing or planning skills may find themselves working to communicate with donors or helping plan an event. In addition, managers have the role of reminding their staff that fundraising is an essential part of each person's job.

The executive director and management staff have a responsibility on the team to create an atmosphere in the organization that is both supportive and motivational in regard to fundraising and all other staff-related work activities. Unless staff believe in their work and are committed to the nonprofit's mission, it will be difficult to interest them in raising funds and participating as part of a larger team effort.

Nonboard Volunteers

Nonboard volunteers play an essential part in providing services in many nonprofits. All too often, nonprofits overlook the fact that these volunteers can also play an essential part in fundraising. In some nonprofits, volunteers have a primary role in fundraising. These are the auxiliaries, speaker's bureaus, major donor committees, and in some cases advisory boards.

TABLE 4.1

Fundraising Team Responsibilities Matrix

Who	What
Leadership Group	
Board Chairperson	• Sets the example for the full board in terms of performance. • Builds commitment among board members and makes sure that the skills and experience of board members are matched to the tasks they perform. • Remains conscious that fundraising is only one of the essential duties of the board of directors.
Executive Director	• Sets an example for the rest of the staff in terms of performance. • Creates enthusiasm about goals, builds commitment among staff to raise funds, and effectively matches skills and experience to the tasks that need to be achieved. • Focuses on the staff's performance. • Often manages the process of team selection and ensures effectiveness of the team.
Development Director or Board Development Chair; Other Leadership Group Members	• Focus primarily on fundraising. • Assist the board chair and executive director to build commitment among team members. • Ensure that adequate research and planning are done, find appropriate technology, and develop written communication. • Coordinate and may facilitate the leadership group meetings.
Other Fundraising Team Members	
Board of Directors	• Accept training to increase skills and become more effective. • Identify: Provide names of colleagues, businesses, etc. • Cultivate: Serve on task forces, matching interests and skills. • Ask: Obtain donations and give donations themselves. • Recognize: Thank donors for their generosity. • Monitor: Set fundraising policies with staff.
Staff	• Accept training to increase skills and become more effective. • Identify: See every contact as a potential donor; track donor data. • Cultivate: Are best source of information about constituent needs, service quality, and programs that are making a difference in the community; are key to demonstrating those positive results and therefore providing a reason for donors to give; communicate to potential and current donors that their non-profit is operating smoothly and is professionally managed. • Ask: Visit with donors and prospects to provide details of their work. • Recognize: Thank donors they know for their generosity.

(Continued)

TABLE 4.1 *Continued*

Nonboard Volunteers
- Accept training to increase skills and become more effective.
- Identify: Introduce their places of employment to the nonprofit to generate contributions; develop list of contacts for solicitations; maintain the donor database; research prospective donors.
- Cultivate: Serve on task forces according to interest and skills.
- Ask: Solicit friends, family, work colleagues, and neighbors to become donors; organize special events; make financial contributions themselves.
- Recognize: Thank donors they know for their gifts.

Whether they come to nonprofits to assist with services or fundraising, they hold a special role on the team because of their close relationship with the community and their nonpaid, essential relationship with the nonprofit.

Nonboard volunteers participate on the fundraising team in many ways. They introduce their places of employment to the nonprofit to generate contributions. They ask friends, family, work colleagues, and neighbors to become donors. They maintain the donor database, research prospective donors, and organize special events. They also make financial contributions themselves.

It is the responsibility of the development director or board fundraising committee chair to make sure that volunteers are an integral part of the team. Building commitment for the goals of the team, clarifying volunteer responsibilities on the team, and ensuring good communication between volunteers and other team players are the tasks that promote strong performance.

Establishing Team Roles

For a team approach to fundraising to work well in any nonprofit, a good understanding among all the members of the team regarding roles is essential. It is best to develop a brief matrix, such as that shown in Table 4.1, that gives a short summation of key team member roles in fundraising. Members of the leadership group have some very specific responsibilities of which to be aware. Other team members can determine their responsibilities in the four key fundraising areas: identifying donors, cultivating them, asking for contributions, and recognizing donor generosity. I cover these four topics in detail later in the book and provide just an overview here to show the interrelationship of all team members' responsibilities.

The matrix can also be used to help prepare short job descriptions of team members to remind everyone of the essential roles played by everyone in the organization. An example of a job description for the board chairperson as team leader is as follows.

The Eastside Community Action Agency Organizational Fundraising Team

Job Description: Board Chairperson

The board chair serves as the inspiration to other board members for their role in fundraising. To that end, this position must

1. *Assist board members in finding team tasks that are most appropriate for them.*

2. *Take the lead in asking others for contributions and in making a significant financial donation to the Agency.*

3. *Work closely with the executive director to support that position's efforts in working with staff and nonboard volunteers who are fundraising team members.*

4. *Motivate, encourage, and inspire all board members in carrying out their team fundraising tasks.*

5. *Take responsibility to ask inactive board team members to leave the organization.*

There would be similar task descriptions for the executive director, development director or board fundraising committee chair, and the leadership group as a whole. You may also find it practical to have job descriptions for staff, board, and nonboard volunteers. These would be based on the activities described in the matrix in Table 4.1.

Generally, the job descriptions for the fundraising team are developed by those who will be fulfilling the responsibilities. The executive director might have an all-staff meeting to draft the team job description for program, administrative, and management staff. Similarly, the board chair may take time at a board meeting to draft the responsibilities of the board team members. Once drafts are finalized and accepted by those carrying out the tasks, they are reviewed by the leadership group to ensure there are no gaps or overlaps.

After your organization has accepted taking a team approach to fundraising, it generally takes team members a month or two to organize themselves under their new job descriptions. The length of time required is somewhat related to the size of your organization and the number of other pressing matters that take up everyone's time.

Identifying Team Fundraising Skills

The leadership group should find out what experience and skills the team members have in fundraising as the team is being formed. You will also need to find out what people in the organization fear about doing fundraising and what they might consider to be fun. You can do this through personal interviews, surveys, focus groups, or other methods. The important point is to talk to everyone who will be a member of the fundraising team.

Generally, organizations take a peer-to-peer approach to determining fundraising experience and skills. In other words, the board chair or board fundraising committee chair will talk to other board members. The executive director or development director will talk to staff, and a nonboard volunteer in the leadership group will talk to other volunteers.

The following skills inventory will aid you in gathering information from people in your organization.

WORKSHEET 4.1

Team Fundraising Skills Survey

The following list indicates the many skills an organization needs for fundraising. Please check off all the ways you want to help as a team member. Each team member should complete this worksheet and return it to the designated leadership group member.

Team member's name _____

	Will do	Maybe; Ask me	I'd like to learn this skill
Identify Donors			
Provide lists of names.	_____	_____	_____
Research current donors.	_____	_____	_____
Research grant funders.	_____	_____	_____
Input data into the database.	_____	_____	_____
Assist with database management.	_____	_____	_____
Cultivation			
Go and talk to other groups about our organization.	_____	_____	_____
Work on a newsletter task force.	_____	_____	_____
Develop the agency case statement.	_____	_____	_____
Visit foundation and corporate prospects.	_____	_____	_____
Work on a legislative task force.	_____	_____	_____
Recruit new volunteers.	_____	_____	_____
Solicitations			
Organize a major donor drive.	_____	_____	_____
Recruit volunteer solicitors.	_____	_____	_____
Solicit people and groups.	_____	_____	_____
Conduct a phone-a-thon.	_____	_____	_____
Organize a direct mail campaign.	_____	_____	_____
Work on a direct mail campaign.	_____	_____	_____
Draft proposals to prospective funders.	_____	_____	_____

Help plan special events.   _____ _____ _____
Lead an events committee.   _____ _____ _____
Work at the event.   _____ _____ _____

Recognize Donors
  Develop recognition events for donors.   _____ _____ _____
  Write and send donor thank you letters.   _____ _____ _____

Note: *This survey is not all-inclusive. Your team will want to add and subtract skills depending on your needs.*

When the inventory is completed by everyone, the leadership group needs to collate the information and begin organizing task forces based on the fundraising goals and objectives outlined for the year and on the interests of team members. (See Chapter Six on developing goals and objectives.)

Forming the Team—An Example

The environmental nonprofit described in this example was organized ten years ago as a regional nonprofit with a small staff, a large board of directors of forty-five members, and many program-related volunteers who work tirelessly to fulfill the mission.

After several years of government funding, the money dried up and the board suddenly faced a potentially huge deficit within several months. The executive director had been extremely successful in raising government funds and for years had told board members not to worry about fundraising—she would take care of it.

With the pending deficit looming, the board wisely began to worry about fundraising. The executive director (just as wisely) said that two staff could not make up the huge deficit and that the board must get involved. All the excuses mentioned earlier about having no contacts, no time, and no energy were made by board members, and several members stopped coming to board or committee meetings.

It became crystal clear that board fundraising was not going to happen spontaneously. As a result, the board chairperson, executive director, and business committee chair (a board volunteer who carried many of the fundraising coordination duties) became the team leaders and took responsibility for motivating and inspiring a reluctant group.

The team leaders brought three recommendations to the board and staff of this nonprofit. One was that each board member would raise or give $500. Another was that staff would support the board with their own campaign with current donors and funders to match what the board was raising. The final goal was that board members would take on some fundraising tasks to identify and cultivate donors based on their interests or skills and so to provide volunteer support in the absence of a development director.

Most board members agreed to the goals. Those that did not were slowly moved off the board and outside the organization.

Although not every board member raised $500, everyone did participate either by asking, giving, or doing a fundraising-related task. The staff participation in the team effort was also quite successful. What is probably the most important result of the teamwork was the confidence that was built regarding both board and staff's ability to raise funds. For the first time, board members saw fundraising as part of their job, and staff saw the importance of the board and staff working together to create a stronger fundraising performance. Now, as board members who leave are replaced with talented new individuals, the team will become even more capable of generating contributions for this nonprofit.

Summary

After the leadership group is working together, the rest of the fundraising team is formed. Members of this team include

- The board of directors
- All staff
- Nonboard volunteers

Each of these groups brings unique responsibilities to the fundraising team, and everyone in the organization should understand what these roles are. The unique responsibilities are important for everyone to understand so the team coalesces quickly and works together well.

Although team members have unique roles depending on their position, they also work within the team based on their fundraising interests and skills. When team members know how they fit on the team based on their roles, their interests, and their skills, it is remarkably easy to work together and value each other's productivity.

Part Two

Getting the Team Ready

Chapter 5

Focusing the Team

ONCE YOU HAVE DEVELOPED an organizational team with a strong leadership group, your next step is to focus the team by means of a shared fundraising vision and purpose. This is a critical step in team development, since it is important for people working together to have a shared understanding of their work as they begin their efforts. This step is also a very creative one in the process of building a team because it allows for some dreaming about how successful the group can be as fundraisers.

What Is a Vision?

Much has been written and said about the importance of having a clear organizational vision that provides a sense of direction. Both corporations and nonprofits carefully design vision statements as part of their long-range strategic planning process. Leaders in these organizations know that a powerful vision statement that is widely shared by key constituents is a key motivator and driving force for success.

A vision is a realistic future for your organization. It's everyone's dream of success for your nonprofit. Success is measured by how well your organization is doing in achieving your vision and fulfilling your organization's mission. A vision statement is very different from a mission statement, which tells your community your purpose or why you exist.

The vision statement captures everyone's dream of the future on paper so that it serves as a written reminder of where you are headed and how you define success. By having a vision statement, you can also share and discuss it with others to achieve greater buy-in.

The Fundraising Vision Statement

Whereas most organizations are guided by their organizational vision statements, it is less common for organizations to have a fundraising vision statement to inspire their fundraising efforts. A fundraising vision statement is essential for your fundraising program and is a microcosm of your organizational vision. It gives a clear and inspirational message that describes your successful fundraising program. For instance, one nonprofit with which I've worked described their fundraising vision as, "Everyone working together, creatively, to provide sufficient dollars for building our organization's programs and meeting the needs of the community." This organization didn't want just one or two people doing all the fundraising, and they did not want to maintain the status quo. Their vision for fundraising and for their nonprofit is big and inspirational.

When you think about your fund development program, what would you like it to look like in the future? It's OK to dream and to be idealistic about your vision, and it's important to be reasonable and realistic. In order for the vision to be inspiring and motivational, it has to stretch people's imaginations to some extent. It has to present a future that seems attainable and at the same time sets high standards and high ideals.

The following information, paraphrased from Burt Nanus's *Visionary Leadership* (published by Jossey-Bass, 1992), describes the specific properties that are inherent in strong vision statements. I have altered the text to reflect the properties for a fundraising vision statement.

1. The fundraising vision statement is appropriate for the organization and fits well into the organization's history, culture, values; it is consistent with the organization's present situation and gives a realistic and informed assessment of an attainable monetary future.

2. The statement sets standards of excellence and depicts the organization's fundraising team as a responsible community with a sense of integrity that is both strengthening and uplifting.

3. The vision statement clarifies purpose and direction for the fund development program.

4. It is persuasive and credible in defining what the organization wants to accomplish in fundraising, while providing hope and promise for a better tomorrow.

5. The vision statement inspires enthusiasm and encourages commitment by reflecting the needs and aspirations of many team members.

6. The statement is well articulated and easily understood so that those who need to turn the vision into reality can internalize it.

7. It reflects the uniqueness of the organization's fundraising efforts—what it stands for, and what it is able to achieve.

8. The vision statement is ambitious. It may call for sacrifice and emotional investment by team members who are committed to undisputed progress and expanding the organization's horizons.

How to Create a Fundraising Vision Statement

As you can imagine from the above description of vision properties, a whole lot goes into a fundraising vision statement. This isn't something that one or two people, or even the leadership group, sits down and throws together to sell to the rest of the team. There needs to be a thoughtful and sometimes lengthy process whereby every team member participates in some way to craft a shared fundraising vision.

A good way to start is to bring together as many of your fundraising team as possible for a three- to four-hour session to gather input and begin drafting your vision. This might be a regularly scheduled board meeting, with staff and nonboard volunteers also in attendance, that you have devoted to fund-development visioning, or it might be a specially called session. You want everyone present at the meeting to ensure that each person has the opportunity to be heard. This will provide a rich variety of input and create greater buy-in.

Several questions can be asked during this vision meeting that will help you draw out ideas and keep the focus on the task of developing the fundraising vision. If possible, send these questions out in advance to everyone so that people can begin to think about them. This advance planning also gives team members who are unable to attend the meeting an opportunity to respond to the questions.

Here are some questions you can ask to begin shaping your fundraising vision:

WORKSHEET 5.1

Vision Development

- Imagine our organization five years from now.
  What new programs do we have?
  How have our current programs changed?
  Has staff size increased?
  Are we in a new facility? If yes, what does it look like?
- Based on the above image of our organization, what is our budget size in five years?
- What revenue sources are used to meet the expenses of our budget? How much of our revenues come from fundraising?
- What methods are we using to raise funds in five years? Of these methods, which one is used the most? Which one brings in the most money?
- How are we communicating our program successes to our stakeholders in five years?
- How are we involving team members? What are we doing that keeps everyone motivated and inspired?

With this information, you can begin to pull out the key phrases or ideas and begin to build a vision statement. Some organizations have very long fundraising vision statements that may be a full page. Others narrow their statements to one or two sentences. Your organization should have a fundraising vision statement that makes sense for your team. Remember that vision statements should be clear and should be internalized by those who have to turn the vision into a reality.

With a fundraising vision statement, you have a broad-brush view of your fundraising program. It is essential to have this broad-brush view in order to take the next step, which is to create a team mandate. The team mandate gives everyone on the team a sense of why you are doing fundraising in the first place and provides a team framework to guide you toward your vision.

Fundraising-Team Mandate

Your fundraising-team mandate is a written description of the purpose of your team. It is a document that gathers together all the work you have done thus far in building your team.

Although you might think the purpose is as simple as saying "to raise money," usually it is a bit more complex. I suggest that you have a written mandate so everyone is aware of the team purpose. When the mandate is written, it should contain the voices of the people who will be working to fulfill it. You will therefore want to gather as much information as possible about what the purpose might be directly from the folks in your organization.

The mandate also contains a list of team players (as described in Chapter Three) and your team's vision (described earlier in this chapter). The mandate becomes your first team document with a summary of who is on the team, your picture of fundraising success, your purpose of working as a team, and the ground rules that team members will use to work together. It is an essential document for everyone on the team to have because it is sometimes important to revisit the mandate with the group in order to help everyone stay focused on what is important—raising dollars for needed community services.

Developing the Fundraising-Team Mandate

As in creating the fundraising vision statement, the leadership group starts the process of developing the full team mandate. The best way to create a team mandate is first to convene the leadership group to discuss the following questions:

- Why is the fundraising team being formed? How is it essential to the organization?
- What makes our fundraising team unique?
- What are the values of our fundraising team?
- What are the ground rules we should follow as a team?
- Who will see our fundraising-team mandate?

After the leadership group has brainstormed answers to these questions, you may find that new questions emerge or that your brainstorming results in divergent viewpoints. Don't worry. At this point, the leadership group is simply opening the discussion, not coming to any conclusions.

With the information gathered at the initial brainstorming, the leadership group should be able to formulate a set of questions to ask all the team members. These questions can be asked to small groups in larger organizations or through personal interviews in smaller ones. If using small groups, it is generally a good idea to mix board with staff and other nonboard volunteers so you can have a good discussion with many different viewpoints. I highly recommend that the discussion be facilitated by a member of the leadership group who does not also participate in the conversation (that is, does not offer personal viewpoints).

This information-gathering exercise serves two purposes: It optimizes input into the fundraising-team mandate, and people in the organization begin working together as a team. Individuals get to know each other, hear differing views, and have healthy discussions on an important topic.

Following the input from everyone else in the organization, the leadership group should have additional discussions among themselves to reach some consensus on the fundraising-team mandate. The task of drafting a mandate should be given to one or two people, who will then bring the draft back to the leadership group for finalization. Once the mandate is finalized, it should be shared with each member of the fundraising team for their comments, and eventually, approval. Below is an example of a fundraising-team mandate.

A Word About Ground Rules

Anyone who has facilitated a raucous meeting knows the importance of having ground rules. Ground rules establish how the group wants to work together, describe group expectations of each other, and give some boundaries for group behavior. In short, they are essential to positive group behavior.

Ground rules need to be developed and agreed upon by all members of the team, not just the leadership. This joint approach makes it much easier to avoid any subsequent ground-rule rebellions.

A Fundraising-Team Mandate

Name of team: the East Bay Social Services Fundraising Team.

List of team members: the EBSS Board of Directors, EBSS staff, EBSS auxiliary, EBSS volunteers (other than board and auxiliary).

Team vision: Everyone working together, creatively, to provide sufficient dollars for building our organization's programs and meeting the needs of the community.

Team mandate: Our purpose is to work in partnership and promote the diverse talents within our organization as we build relationships with prospective and current donors to achieve our fundraising vision.

Team Ground Rules

1. *We will respect each other's diverse opinions and work together as allies.*

2. *We will make fundraising team decisions by consensus whenever possible.*

3. *We expect each person to participate actively in fundraising and to take on a role that is of interest.*

4. *We will work together, in partnership, to realize our vision. This means that we see both our successes and our disappointments as belonging to the team.*

5. *We will have fun.*

The following worksheet will help your group develop your own team mandate. The leadership group should use this worksheet after they have begun their own discussion on the mandate with the questions described earlier regarding the mandate under "Developing the Fundraising-Team Mandate." The following worksheet is for everyone in the nonprofit to use to give their input as a team member.

WORKSHEET 5.2

Defining the Team's Mandate

List the team members by affiliation (for example, board, staff, etc.).

1.
2.
3.
4.
5.

Describe up to five reasons for having a fundraising team.

1.
2.
3.
4.
5.

What ground rules do you want the team to use as we work together?

1.
2.
3.
4.
5.

You may have other questions you want to use for your own team's mandate. Worksheet 5.2 can be modified to best fit the needs of your organization.

Developing Social Bonds

In addition to facilitating the process of developing a fundraising vision and team mandate, the leadership group should also think of ways to build a strong social bond between individuals who will be on the team. Having a clear vision is important for direction, having a team mandate concretizes purpose, and having a strong social bond is important for team productivity and good morale. It is much easier to get through some of the darker moments of fundraising if everyone goes through them as a group with a good bond to hold them together.

Another reason to build strong social bonds is to help team members see that they have a voice on the team—that they have some influence. Teams in which members feel their ideas are being heard are generally the most successful, especially in fundraising, where creativity counts heavily on whether efforts produce successful results. You need a lot of creative ideas from many diverse people to generate a good fundraising program. If there is a good social bond, individuals will be more willing to speak up and take the risk of suggesting a creative, slightly off-the-wall idea that could be a real winner.

Creating the team's social bond is where leadership groups often don't spend enough time. I have met leaders with the attitude, "We don't have time for social acts—we have work to do." What these leaders fail to understand is that taking some time up front to bring the team together with a strong social mind will make the team more productive. More will be accomplished in less time.

How to Form Team Social Bonds

There are three distinct types of activities to use when designing opportunities for teams to interact socially. The first type of activity is useful as the group is first forming. These are "getting to know you" activities that help team members see each other in new and different ways. These activities are important even in small organizations, where it may seem that everybody knows everyone else in the organization fairly intimately. What "getting to know you" or ice-breaker activities do is open up people's thinking about who their fellow team members are—what they like, what they fear, and what they enjoy (or don't enjoy) about fundraising. As team members learn more about each other, their trust grows, they feel closer to each other, and they coalesce into a committed and resourceful team.

One of the best variations of this type of activity is to get everyone together in a group circle and ask each person to describe why they are involved with (such-and-such) organization, and what excites them about the organization's potential. By asking these questions initially, you are focusing attention on each person's feelings about the organization. It is generally helpful to start off building a team with low-personal-risk questions such as these.

As trust builds, in later discussions you can move into more personal exercises that ask people what they feel is their greatest accomplishment, or what their greatest fundraising fear is, or to talk about how they came to work with the organization.

In large organizations (with over fifty staff, volunteers, and board members), it may be impossible to have everyone sit down in the same room together. In this situation, the leadership group will need to think about who to bring together to develop social bonds throughout the organization. I strongly encourage a mix of board, staff, and nonboard volunteers in a series of team meetings. I also encourage at least one all-organization meeting or social gathering in which everyone can at least introduce themselves so that faces can be put with names.

Soon, team members will begin to interact with one another at a level of trust based on a better understanding of each other. The leadership group should acknowledge that this is happening and celebrate this success. Celebrations are a critical part of building strong social bonds. Many small celebrations each year are better for team building than having one major celebration per year. Celebrating small wins is very important for people because they can see their progress and be inspired to do more.

Small-win celebrations are the second way to build strong social bonds. During the year (or over a number of years during a capital campaign), as your organization's fund-raising plan is being executed, there will be ups and downs. Successes, such as major donations received and grants awarded, fuel the enthusiasm of board, staff, and volunteer alike, while disappointments can derail (I hope only temporarily) your organization's fundraising efforts. It is important, therefore, for members of the fund development team to take time out to celebrate the team's successes and regroup after disappointments.

Fundraising *is* hard work. Remember that simple fact. Everyone involved in a nonprofit's fundraising activities needs to be applauded for doing a job well—for writing personal notes on annual fund letters, helping secure a grant from a local family foundation, participating in a year-long cultivation of an individual that results in a major gift, and so on.

All members of the fundraising team need to be apprised of such successes, and acknowledgments need to be made. One suggestion for keeping members of the fundraising team informed is through an internal newsletter or information sheet produced by either the development director or a volunteer. It should be kept very simple. Items can be in bullets. And this newsletter can either be mailed or sent via the Internet.

Celebrate more significant milestones in other ways. Throw an informal party when you achieve 50 percent of your annual fund campaign goal or exceed the targeted goal for new members. Post a sign outside your facility, using an arrow, thermometer, or other visual device that shows your agency's fundraising progress. As the arrow moves up, it will visually inform a broader community constituency that you are well on your way to meeting your nonprofit's fundraising goal.

Bringing everyone together for small-win celebrations builds team confidence in fundraising and also strengthens the social bond. Team members who may not see each other regularly have an opportunity to make connection and enjoy their time together.

You don't always need a small win to bring the team together. The third type of team-building social activity is get-togethers, such as potlucks, picnics, bowling, softball games, or any number of other activities in which team members can interact. These events should be optional (you shouldn't force team members to be social). The idea, though, is to make them so much fun that everyone will want to participate.

If you take the time to help your team members get to know each other and join together for small wins and social activities, you will form a stronger team. Members will be generally happier about their fundraising tasks and look to each other for support. Your celebrations will reinforce the idea that fundraising successes are a win for the whole team and that it takes the whole organization to make fundraising successful. You will also find that you have a more productive team that is spending less time resisting the fundraising tasks that need to be accomplished.

What to do if . . . What happens if the newly formed team begins to flounder? First, don't panic. It is natural for teams to have their ups and downs. The leadership group will need to step in quickly when they begin to see team members losing interest or motivation, or when tasks are not being completed. Bring the fundraising team together, talk about what's happening, and assess how things can be improved. If necessary, revise goals. Perhaps the original ones were too ambitious at this particular time.

Another suggestion is to ask the most inspirational member of the fundraising team to give everyone a pep talk. Or bring in an outside expert whose words of wisdom and experience can serve as a breath of fresh air to weary and beleaguered team members.

Typically, it is the team's leadership group who must motivate and encourage other team members (other board members, staff, and nonboard volunteers) when spirits are flagging. This group must be sensitive to the fact that board members and volunteers are not getting paid to do the hard, challenging work of fundraising for an organization.

And though staff members are usually compensated for their work (albeit often not nearly enough for the long, stressful hours on the job), they, too, need kudos and encouragement from time to time.

Summary

This chapter describes how to begin focusing your fundraising team with a shared fundraising vision and mandate. The team fundraising vision describes everyone's picture of success for the team; the fundraising mandate defines the purpose of the team and the ground rules everyone agrees to use while working together.

As the team begins to focus, it is important to stay conscious of building and strengthening strong social bonds for the group. This chapter gives several examples to help you undertake the important activity of developing a group that is productive and enjoys working together to achieve its vision and goals.

The next chapter builds on the team's fundraising vision, mandate, and social bonds, and discusses setting team goals through organizationwide fundraising planning. My premise is that it takes clear goals and specific tasks to move the team forward to achieve the fundraising vision.

Chapter 6

Setting Fundraising Goals and Objectives

WITH THE FUNDRAISING VISION clarified and your mandate set, it is time to take the next step of setting your course with goals and objectives to form the base of your strategic fundraising plan. Clear team fundraising goals and objectives help members know when they are achieving those small wins described in the previous chapter. The strategic plan, with its team goals and objectives, also helps you evaluate how successful you have been. In this chapter I define fundraising goals and objectives and move you through a process of developing them into a strategic fundraising plan.

Organizationwide Strategic Planning

As you set fundraising goals and objectives and develop a fundraising plan, it's important to understand that fundraising team goals should tie to your organization's overall strategic plan. It is far easier to raise money for an organization that can justify their financial needs based on identified long-term program and operations goals. Having a clear organizational plan gives credibility and validity to your fundraising.

If you already have an organizational strategic plan in place, the leadership group should distribute copies to all team members to use while developing the fundraising plan with its goals and objectives.

Let's say you don't have an organizationwide strategic plan, as is not that uncommon in nonprofits. What do you do? Conduct a short strategic planning process as a team-building effort whereby the entire organization creates or recommits to your mission statement and develops long-term program and administration priorities.

In a small organization (with a few staff members, some key volunteers, and a board of twelve to fifteen members) this can be done in a one-day retreat organized by the leadership group. In larger organizations, the leadership group may need to survey some staff and volunteers and have a retreat with just management staff and board members. So it will take a while longer with larger organizations. Taking the extra time to establish long-term priorities for the whole organization, however, is a key step to ensuring fundraising success, and is well worth the effort.

Also, don't do organizational planning in a vacuum. Find an interested team member or a small group within the team to conduct an external trend analysis to determine the changes that are occurring in the demographic, economic, cultural, environmental, and technological arenas in your target population. This step is important because you need to make sure your programs and services will continue to meet your community's needs as you go forward. No one wants to give a contribution to an organization that has obsolete programs, so studying what is changing in your population helps you stay vital, and helps you bring in donations.

If you have never conducted a strategic planning process, you might find the following two books very helpful. They are both workbooks and give good step-by-step instructions to creating a plan for your organization. I recommend *Strategic Planning for Nonprofit Organizations,* by Jude Kaye and Michael Allison (1997, Wiley). I also recommend the *Strategic Planning Workbook,* by Bryan Barry (published by Amherst Wilder Foundation, 1997).

Fundraising Goals and Objectives— The Planning Process

With a good organizationwide strategic plan in place, it becomes easier to develop a fundraising plan with concrete goals and objectives. Developing this plan requires several phases. The first phase is to analyze what is currently working well in fundraising and what is not working well. You will also want to include the external trend analysis you did as part of your strategic planning, since trends may affect your ability to raise money. When this analysis phase is concluded, you will move into phase two, which is the development of a fundraising plan with goals, objectives, and tasks that build on your fundraising strengths and transform your weaknesses into strengths, while paying careful attention to the important trends. A part of this second phase is also writing the plan and getting team approval of it. The third phase is implementation, which puts the team into action and moves them toward meeting the goals and objectives. This entire process is led by the leadership group with full input from the rest of the team.

Analyzing What Is Already Working Well in Fundraising

This phase provides the base for building a solid fundraising plan. In what areas have you already had success with fundraising? What are the strengths in your organization that can be used for fundraising? What are the organizational weaknesses that need to be addressed so you may be more successful in fundraising? What are the financial needs for the year that should be addressed through fundraising?

Conducting a brief internal fund development audit annually provides an organization with a good picture of what to focus fundraising on. With a fundraising team, you are relieved of having a single staff person doing the entire analysis and can ensure that multiple perspectives are considered.

The leadership group oversees the whole process and makes sure the results are shared with the team. The group identifies board members, staff, and nonboard volunteers who have skills in analysis and asks them to conduct a fundraising audit. This small group asks board members to give their ideas on strengths and weaknesses. Board members also help identify the organization's priorities for the year and determine the financial needs. Accounting staff provide details on fund development activities that have worked and those that have not been successful. Program staff help identify the financial needs of their programs. Fundraising volunteers may provide a community perspective on the strengths and weaknesses of the organization. Everyone thus has a role in analyzing current fund development efforts and completing this first important step.

When the information has been gathered, the development director, or in organizations where there is not a designated development person, the executive director, or another member of the leadership group organizes the information into a report.

I've included Worksheet 6.1 to help team members provide input to the process of determining what fundraising activities have been successful in the past and present.

WORKSHEET 6.1

Fund Development Analysis

1. List your sources of income over the past three years by category (for example, foundations, corporations, special events, fee for service, major donors). Include names of institutional funders, and break down other categories in as much detail as you can.

2. Of these sources, which have increased financially in the past three years and which have decreased? What are the reasons for any decreases?

3. Have any of your financial sources grown in size (larger events, more phone calls in a telephone campaign, for instance) but not in income? In other words, are you spending more but raising less?

4. Determine available resources for fundraising, including

   Staff

   Money

   Equipment

   Volunteers (including board members)

   Knowledge and skills

5. Does your donor tracking system give you the information you need to cultivate and ask appropriately?

6. What are the organizational priorities for the next year? Will fundraising need to increase to achieve these priorities?

7. Do your programs and operations have financial needs that must be met by fundraising? What are those needs?

8. Would you describe your organization's visibility in your community as high, medium, or low? Why?

9. Are you well perceived by your community? If not, what must you do to gain respect and credibility?

10. What information from the trend analysis will have an impact on your fundraising efforts?

    Specifically, look at

    Community demographics

    Economics

    Cultural patterns

    Technology

    Environment

11. Summarize the opportunities in the community that you feel will help your fundraising (based on trends) and the barriers to fundraising success you can identify through the trends.

12. With all this information, what are the major fundraising strengths in your organization and what are the weaknesses?

You may want to spend some time at board and staff meetings and with nonboard volunteers to brainstorm the nonfinancial questions in the worksheet. The following criteria can be used to help measure whether an organization is in a position of strength or weakness as it raises funds. For an organization to be at its best with fundraising, the following general criteria should be in place.

- Strong organization mission and vision known by stakeholders and reflected by the organization

- Programs, services, and advocacy work that are viewed by the community as essential

- A positive reputation in the community

- Interested and involved constituents who support the work of the organization

- Systems in place that accurately track donations and monitor progress

- Strategies that are practiced for cultivating and recognizing donors

- A board of directors, staff, and volunteers who are actively engaged in practicing a team approach to fundraising

With the information from this brainstorming session, the team can move into a discussion at later meetings regarding financial priorities of the organization. Program staff will have met with the executive director and other staff to draft financial needs for the coming year, and these will be presented to the board for discussion and approval prior to finalizing the annual budgeting.

Developing the Fundraising Plan— Setting Goals and Objectives

When the board and staff have agreed on financial priorities for the year and have clarified organizational strengths and weaknesses and external trends, it is time to set your fundraising goals and objectives and organize these into a fundraising plan. Remember that a fundraising plan is your roadmap to financial success both in terms of bringing needed dollars into the organization and in turning some of the weaknesses identified in the fundraising audit into strengths.

The best way to create a fundraising plan is to have a brainstorming session with team members first. Team members should first be asked to read the fundraising analysis report prepared by the leadership group. Then the full team can come together with someone from the leadership group to facilitate the brainstorming. To help with the brainstorming, you can use the following worksheet with the group:

WORKSHEET 6.2

Setting Fundraising Goals and Objectives

Identifying Donors
- What markets should be cultivated and solicited?
- Are there current donors who should be giving more?
- What new information do we want to track on our prospects and donors?

Cultivating Donors
- What are our tried-and-true cultivation techniques that we should continue?
- What new cultivation techniques should we consider, based on donor needs and agency resources?

Soliciting Donors
- What are our tried-and-true fundraising methods that we should continue?
- What new fundraising ideas should we try?
- How much do we need to raise this year to support our programs and operations?

Recognizing Donors
- What recognition activities should we continue to use this year?

Fundraising Systems
- What additional accounting or database systems are needed to support fundraising?
- What new marketing activities should we pursue?

Forming the Plan
- Based on the answers to the above questions, what are our fundraising goals for the year?
- What are the measurable (monthly or quarterly) objectives we will use to ensure that we reach these goals?
- What activities are the best ones (based on our strengths and weaknesses) to use to reach these objectives?

Each organization may have additional questions that need to be answered based on the findings from their analysis. Remember that the essential idea of the brainstorming session is to get team players involved in the planning at the earliest stages so that buy-in will be more likely once the plan is in place.

After some good brainstorming, the leadership group should meet to draft the goals and objectives for the fundraising plan and then put everything together into one document.

Exhibit 6.1 is a generic table of contents for a fundraising plan. You can use it to help develop one for your organization.

In addition to monetary goals and objectives, sections of your plan should include raising of money to support team development, board development, technology, marketing, and volunteer recruitment.

When the draft is completed, the leadership group should present it to the rest of the team. This might be in a meeting with the full team to gain

---

EXHIBIT 6.1

Fundraising Plan Table of Contents

- Fundraising vision and mandate
- Organizationwide annual program and administrative priorities
- Fundraising goals and objectives for the year
- Action plan to achieve goals and objectives
- Fundraising budget

---

input on the plan from board members, staff, and nonboard volunteers. Or, in larger organizations, there might be a series of meetings. The best way to do this is for the executive director to meet with staff team members and get their input. The executive director might also meet with the nonboard volunteers, unless these individuals are working more closely with the board of directors. The board chairperson meets with the rest of the board to talk about the plan.

When the fundraising plan has been accepted, team members should organize themselves to decide upon and carry out the activities. Certain team members will feel more comfortable researching, identifying, and tracking prospects. Others will enjoy cultivating donors, while still others will be more comfortable in asking for contributions. Most, if not all, team members should enjoy the thanking of donors for their generosity. Team members should decide initially which areas(s) they want to participate in and should be free to do activities that they enjoy most.

The next section of this book describes in more detail the ways to organize the team members to put the team into action.

A Word on Goals and Objectives

There are probably as many definitions of goals and objectives as there are planners. To ensure that we are speaking the same language, here are the definitions that I'm using in this book.

A *goal* is what you want to accomplish in some distant future. That distant time could be as short as a year if you are just getting started with a fundraising plan or have difficulties seeing beyond a year. Other groups may try to set goals for three to five years, depending on the time frame of their strategic plan.

An *objective* is a shorter-term benchmark that tells the team what you intend to accomplish along the way to reaching your goals. Objectives should be measurable, outcome-oriented, and time-referenced so that they are truly benchmarks.

In a fundraising plan, you may have a few broad goals with several objectives for each goal that indicate where your progress should be at certain points along the way to reaching your goals. If your team is taking a comprehensive approach to fundraising, your goals and objectives will probably cover the four main areas of fundraising (identifying prospective donors, cultivating them, asking for donations, and recognizing contributions).

For instance, let's say you have a goal of increasing foundation giving by 50 percent of the current giving levels in three years. You might then have a six-month objective of obtaining three new foundation grants of $5,000 each or more. There would be additional benchmarks for every six-month level along the way to the three-year goal.

Creating a Fundraising Plan—An Example

Here's an example of how this planning process worked in a large nonprofit that had a small staff and a great many volunteers (not all of them board members).

The executive director, board chair, board fundraising committee chair, and a key fundraising volunteer (not on the board) met with staff, board, and other volunteers over a period of four months to outline a fundraising plan. This small group analyzed what could reasonably be raised through membership acquisition and renewal, foundation and corporate grants, government contracts, and events. They drafted realistic goals for anticipated growth in fundraising. They focused one goal on marketing the organization, since this was a current weakness. Financial objectives were based on previous experience and a changing political climate that meant that fewer government dollars were going to be available for programs.

As goals, objectives, and activities were discussed, other staff and board members were brought into the meetings to help determine tasks that all team members would be happy with for the year. Everyone agreed that board, staff, and volunteers together would jointly share the responsibility for carrying out the activities and meeting the objectives. When the plan was presented to the rest of the team, it was accepted with a few modifications.

The leadership group took responsibility for organizing small task forces of team members (sometimes only two people) to accomplish each activity and worked with everyone to monitor and ensure that everyone did their work. For instance, with foundations and corporations, a person in the leadership group provided oversight and worked with several of the team to complete activities such as researching potential funders, contacting them for materials, preparing proposals, going on visits to funders who had received proposals, and doing other follow-up. In each of these activities, board, staff, and nonboard volunteers participated.

Reports were made at board meetings and staff meetings about progress made toward meeting the specific objectives of the fundraising plan. When problems arose, the task force contacted the leadership group and the problems were worked out. By the end of the year, the organization had met or exceeded all of its fundraising objectives and had a strong team of board, staff, and nonboard volunteers who were eager to get started on the next year. The process was effective largely because team members were involved in setting the priorities for the year and in the planning to raise funds to meet those priorities. Team members understood why they were raising funds and how the funds would be used.

Planning Time Line

Sometimes when a team-oriented planning approach is recommended to organizations, I hear a collective groan that such a process takes way too long and funds are needed now. This hesitancy is understandable. When an organization does use a team approach to fundraising, it may take several months the first year to get organized and do the planning. However, once the pattern is set, the planning process moves very quickly. Expect to take four to five months doing some planning as a full team while you are also working together to develop job descriptions, determine a vision and mandate, and build social bonds.

Summary

With a good fundraising plan in place, a team always knows who is doing what, and they have objectives by which to measure their progress. Strong motivation often comes from having clear objectives and a clear definition of how to achieve them. Team members know they are not alone in doing fundraising, and they understand their own particular responsibilities for achieving success.

Chapter 7
Training the Team

TRAINING THE TEAM for fundraising success begins early in the process, right after the team begins taking shape. Preparation lays a solid foundation for building fundraising success, especially for board members and other volunteers who will participate in an organization's fundraising efforts. Therefore, this chapter outlines the steps that should occur before an "ask" is ever made.

Fundraising Orientation

The leadership group should hold an orientation program as the team is forming. An orientation program not only helps bring team members "up to speed" on the agency and its work, but it also serves to remind team members why fundraising is so important. Orientation sessions provide the agency's fundraising leadership group with the opportunity to motivate and reenergize the board.

Generally, the most useful orientation sessions cover topics such as a summary of the nonprofit agency's history, an overview of the field of service (for example, arts, environment, education, homelessness), a description of the agency's programs, a review of the financial condition of the organization, current fundraising activities, and information on current donors.

One nonprofit organization I have worked with holds a special orientation meeting for all team members, new and current, each year. In this orientation, new board members learn more about the nonprofit, staff members describe what they do and their respective duties and responsibilities, and nonboard volunteers describe their work as well.

What fundraising information should be provided at an orientation session? The short answer—a snapshot of the recent past and a blueprint for the agency's immediate future. By *snapshot* I mean information that summarizes key facts and figures about the nonprofit agency's recent fundraising history. Snapshot materials show the sources and amounts of the agency's revenues (that is, earned and fee-for-service income; grants from government agencies, corporations, and foundations; individual contributions; and monies netted from special events). To make this information more easily understandable to your team, depict this data graphically—for example, in the form of a pie chart or graph. It may also be advisable to use percentages as well as actual dollars.

It may be instructive for team members to see the number of gifts received within the various donor categories (that is, dollar ranges) for each funding source. For example, how many $1,000–plus gifts were received from individuals? How many individual gifts between $500 and $999? How many corporate or foundation grants at $10,000? At $5,000?

This level of detail quickly educates new and continuing team members on the annual sources and amounts of contributed money. And when depicted on a graph or chart, it is easier to see both the strengths and challenges of an organization's fundraising program.

How to Set Up the Team Orientation

As the team is beginning to coalesce with its vision, mandate, and plan, the leadership group should organize the orientation. Some organizations integrate team orientation with the planning process, whereas others have the orientation as a separate activity. Regardless, ensuring that team members understand the current status of their organization is essential to fundraising success.

Usually the person who is the most detail-oriented takes on the task of organizing an orientation. In a very large organization, you may need to plan two or three orientations to accommodate everyone. In smaller organizations, everyone can generally get together at the same time.

The first time a team does an orientation for the group may last as long as three hours because there is much to discuss. If you have annual orientations (as I recommend), subsequent sessions will often be finished in two hours.

It is usually a good idea to run the orientation as a social gathering as well as a discussion of the current status of the organization. Planning the meeting around lunch or dinner is a good way to make it more social. Holding a social "happy hour" after the orientation is also a good way for team members to get to know one another better.

Exhibit 7.1 provides you with an agenda for an orientation that I recently had for a newly formed team. I caution that this agenda and its time frames worked very well for this nonprofit, but it is only an example of what can be done at an orientation.

EXHIBIT 7.1

Fundraising Team Generic Orientation Agenda (assumes full team attendance)

I.   Introductions of team members
     Usually done with an ice breaker in which each person talks briefly about what they do and why they joined the organization.
II. Organization overview (usually done by the executive director)
     • Program and facility descriptions
     • Organization staffing chart
     • Financial picture
     • Fundraising plan
III. Review of team vision, mandate, and responsibilities (usually done by board chair)
IV. Team expectations (full group discussion)
     • What team members expect from each other
     • What team members expect from themselves
V.   Orientation wrap-up (usually done by board chair)
     • Task force sign-ups
     • Final questions from new members

Year-Round Training

The team orientation is only the first step in training everyone to be successful fundraisers. When the team orientation is complete, everyone will have a good understanding of your organization and your current fundraising activities. The next step is to provide ongoing training for everyone on the fundraising team—board members, nonboard volunteers, and staff—in identifying, cultivating, asking, and recognizing donors. And remember: Just as successful fundraising is a year-round process, so too should fundraising training take place consistently throughout the year.

Fundraising education and training can take several forms. Many fine books and articles have been written about fundraising topics—from soliciting major donors and planning successful fundraising events to implementing planned giving programs. A good development director, or other team members interested in fundraising, will keep abreast of new trends in the field by reading the current literature and sharing the most important information with others on the fundraising team.

Training sessions and workshops, especially those that incorporate hands-on experience, are especially effective in introducing team members to basic fundraising concepts and techniques while dispelling some commonly-held myths. And they also offer a real opportunity to turn team players into team leaders.

The best way to start the training process is for one or more members of the leadership group to survey team members to find out what they want to learn more about. The following sample survey will help the leadership group take this step.

EXHIBIT 7.2

Survey Questions

1. What aspects of fundraising would you like to know more about?
2. What are some strengths and weaknesses you see on the team that could be improved upon with training?
3. What fears do you have about fundraising that training could help you overcome?
4. What training could help you manage defensiveness and feelings of rejection?
5. Do you prefer to have outside trainers come to our organization or to go to workshops already scheduled in the community?
6. Are there any topics in team-building training you would like us to have?

Your survey results will help the leadership group determine the types of training needed. Depending on the needs, the size of the organization, and the budgeted amount for training, you may decide to bring in someone for a series of workshops on the topics of interest to your team members, or you may send team members to general fundraising workshops held in your community.

It's very important to allow those team members who have already said they will "only send out thank you letters" to obtain training that might help them learn how to ask for contributions, research grant funders, prepare a newsletter, or stimulate whatever other interest that person might have. Remember that one of the joys of being a team member is learning new skills and broadening interests. The leadership group can, of course, ask anyone who attends any training to come back and share their newly learned knowledge with other members of the team so that everyone benefits.

Fundraising training should not be used as a performance incentive. Team members should receive training in aspects of fundraising, regardless of how well they are doing on their jobs. Following this recommendation helps eliminate a situation in which some team members feel less a part of the group because they are not receiving the same benefits. In this case, the benefit is training.

It is often helpful to set up a training calendar, especially if you are in a large organization and there has been a lot of interest in different fundraising topics. A calendar helps the whole team see what training is available throughout a month or year. Generally, someone in the leadership group will take responsibility for setting up the calendar, researching training opportunities and costs, and making sure the calendar is distributed. Table 7.1 presents a sample annual calendar of opportunities for fundraising training for an organization.

TABLE 7.1

Fundraising Training Calendar

Fiscal or Calendar Year

Year Begins	Month Two	Month Three	Month Four
• Team orientation	• Donor research training (offered by fundraising group)	• Major donor training—first session (in-house)	• Major donor training—second session (in-house)

Month Five	Month Six	Month Seven	Month Eight
• Proposal writing training	• Major donor training—first session (in-house) repeat	• Donor research training (offered by fundraising group) repeat • Major donor training—second session (in-house) repeat	• Special events training (offered by fundraising group)

Month Nine	Month Ten	Month Eleven	Month Twelve
• Brochure, newsletter development by (offered nonprofit training services)		• Next year's training needs identified	

Team Fundraising Training—An Example

Cheryl Clarke contributed this story about a public library foundation, on the eve of its first-ever capital campaign, that held a series of fundraising workshops conducted by an outside consultant. The campaign goal was ambitious: $3 million. The campaign leadership team (comprising the head librarian, the chair of the board of trustees, and a volunteer) knew that the library needed the commitment of hundreds of volunteer fundraisers in order to be successful.

Trustees, senior members of the library's staff, and Friends of the Library were invited to attend the workshops. The Friends are a dedicated group of volunteers, many of them seniors, who assist the small, overworked library staff in cataloging and shelving books. The Friends group also organizes periodic library book sales that raises modest sums of money to support additional library services not covered in the budget.

One of the workshops was attended by a woman in her mid-seventies, a friend of the library whose previous fundraising experience consisted solely of volunteering at the library's regular book sales. During the introductions at the beginning of the day, she confessed that while loving the library and wanting to support its capital campaign, she questioned whether she would ever feel comfortable in asking anyone for money. Gamely, she agreed to stay through the day. She listened attentively during the morning presentation that focused on getting the group knowledgeable about the library's case for support. The trainer also emphasized the need for volunteers to build relationships with potential donors.

The afternoon session was devoted to a role-playing exercise in which workshop participants were asked to practice conducting face-to-face solicitations in front of the entire group. Three volunteers were needed at a time, one to play the potential library donor and the other two to make the solicitation. One by one, participants volunteered until only this woman and a few others remained.

Mustering her courage, the elderly woman stepped forward and delivered the most passionate, compelling case for support of the library campaign presented that day. Later, smiling at her own accomplishment, the woman said that the workshop had demystified the entire fundraising process. She came to realize that the library needed the participation of people like her—individuals in the community who are passionate about their beloved public library—in order to reach the campaign goal of $3 million. An effective training session had converted a loyal, but fearful, supporter into a fundraising team leader.

This case study is important for two reasons. First, it illustrates how effective training can help demystify the fundraising process and motivate even the most reluctant of team members. Second, it shows the team concept in action. Senior staff members participated in the training sessions. The library's fundraising leadership team knew that the library would need to use all of its personnel resources to raise the $3 million. Therefore, they brought branch librarians, reference librarians, and others into the process early on. During the campaign, each played a key role in cultivating and soliciting gifts.

Summary

The following outline shows how team members can participate in the training of the entire fund development team.

Team Tasks for Training

Everyone

- Participates actively and consistently in the training to implement the fundraising plan

- Offers suggestions for training topics

- Stays up-to-date on current fundraising trends and issues

Leadership group or training task force

- Develops and implements relevant fundraising training programs

- Creates and distributes training calendars for all team members

- Polls team members for new training opportunities

- Ensures that there is a budget for fundraising training

- Distributes relevant fundraising literature among team members

Part Three

The Team in Action

Chapter 8

Identifying Potential Donors

EVERYONE ON THE TEAM can participate in identifying potential new donors, that is, individuals who are interested in, respect, and value an agency's work. No one should waste precious time and energy trying to convert a passionate classical music lover (and chamber orchestra supporter) into an equally passionate animal welfare enthusiast. In this case, energy should be focused on identifying others who value organizations that exist to help animals.

Identifying External Prospects

There are many ways to locate good donors not currently involved in your organization and many ways to stimulate team members to get involved in identifying them. I present one way, and suggest you let the creative minds in your own organizations think of others.

One socially oriented activity is to gather the team together for a two-hour session and have everyone pull out their Rolodexes listing friends, colleagues, relatives, businesses they use, and acquaintances. The leadership group of the fundraising team should encourage board members, volunteers, and staff members to review their address books and larger circle of acquaintances, coworkers, and neighbors to identify individuals who are most likely to support their agency. If your agency has a development director, he or she will often spearhead this effort on behalf of the leadership team.

Please note that I include staff members in this step of the fundraising process. Too frequently staff are overlooked, as many organizations seem to think that only their boards and nonboard volunteers are "connected" to potential donors. This simply isn't true. Staff members know people too.

Tapping into their energy and enthusiasm is an important resource that members of the fundraising team should not overlook when developing a prospect list.

The board chair should set an example by producing his or her own list of prospects and by emphasizing the importance of this step to fellow board members. Then the leadership group should stress to everyone else on the team that prospects are found, not made. Then it's time to start scanning those Rolodexes.

The team member facilitating the meeting can ask several questions to help everyone in the identification process. Here are some sample questions.

- Who do you generally talk to about this organization?

- Who might want to be involved because they have a personal interest in the mission, or because they have an interest in what you are doing?

- Who might have some extra money and may not have a plan for their charitable gifts?

- Who has had a previous relationship with your nonprofit but is no longer involved?

- Who benefits from what we do?

Worksheet 8.1 will help you with this activity. Each team member gets the worksheet (or several copies of it) to identify whom they know and the possible giving levels for that person, company, or other prospect.

WORKSHEET 8.1

Donor Identification Worksheet

Prospect Name, Address, and Phone	Agency Connection	Interests	Donation Level	Contact Person

It's also important to realize that having one gathering of team members to search Rolodexes is not enough to build a strong prospective donor list. One or more team members should manage a computerized database of donors and prospects. Anyone on the team who thinks of a potential new donor should go to these designated team members to give them the new prospect's name and address. Often the database management team members are staff, but not always. Depending on the size of your organization and the skills of your team members, you may have board members or nonboard volunteers who are actively managing your database if staffing this area is not possible.

To make identifying external donor prospects a social gathering as well as an important fundraising activity, the leadership group should encourage interactions between people to compare whom they know. You might also have a fun-oriented contest to see who can fill out the most worksheets.

Internal Prospects

Another way to identify prospective donors is for some of the more detail-oriented team members to form a task force to review your current organizational mailing lists and donor records for individuals, foundations, companies, and other contributors who may be able to upgrade their contributions. Remember, in fundraising, there are at least three levels of donors: those making their first gift to the organization, those making a repeat gift, and those making a major gift. Researching current donor lists helps find donors who might make a repeat gift or could be part of a major donor campaign.

When the donor research task force has compiled their lists of who might make a gift and for what amount, these lists can be given to whomever on the team is taking the lead in cultivation.

It's important that the task force for researching prospective donors understand that this is an on-going process. You may want to set up a quarterly schedule to review donor lists and the activity of that quarter to see whether new repeat or major donors emerge from these lists.

Also, don't forget about the possibility of team members as prospective donors. It is much easier to participate in fundraising in a nonprofit when you are already a donor to that organization. Board members, staff, and nonboard volunteers should all recognize that they are prospective donors and give generously.

Evaluating and Tracking Prospective Donors

In your search for prospective donors, you will probably find some who need individual attention as prospective major donors and others who can receive a mass appeal for a contribution. Worksheet 8.1, which team members use in the general brainstorming session for new prospects, is an ideal tool for beginning to evaluate particular individuals whom you want to cultivate carefully as a potential major donor.

The same worksheet can be used by team members who are sorting through your current donor database. There may be less information available on the interests of these donors, since they may not be personally known by those doing the research. However, information can be added as cultivation progresses with these prospects.

As worksheets are completed, the information should be added to a prospect database managed by team members. Sort out the prospects who may be major donor material and have a separate section of the database devoted to this group.

Sometimes a communication glitch occurs between team members who maintain the database with "hot prospects" and the team members who cultivate them. A good system should be in place whereby updated lists of prospects are given to cultivation team members who are responsible for educating and communicating with major donors. At the same time, it is important for those of you actively cultivating major donor prospects to provide updates on interests, donation levels, and so forth to help keep lists up to date. If your organization uses e-mail actively, keeping everyone informed should be relatively simple. If e-mail is still in your future, you may want to set up monthly or quarterly summaries to be given to all appropriate team members.

Identifying Donors—An Example

An executive director (and only staff member) of a small social services agency had been carefully training and preparing her twelve-member board of directors and several nonboard volunteers to do some major fundraising for a significant new program. She and her leadership group members, consisting of the board chair, the fundraising committee chair, and a nonboard volunteer, set the agenda for a two-hour meeting in which all board members and several nonboard volunteers were to gather and identify everyone they knew who might give money for this program. Everyone was asked to bring address books, Rolodexes, and creative energy to the meeting.

The executive director went through the current donor list and prepared a list of all individuals, foundations, and corporations who might have an interest. This was sent out to attendees ahead of the meeting so that everyone could identify whom they knew on the list and to ensure there was not a duplication of names. People were also given several of the donor identification worksheets to write down names of everyone who was not already a donor of this organization. These were sent back to the executive director prior to the meeting and compiled into a master list.

When the group arrived for the meeting, they were given the master list of current donors and prospects added by team members. The first part of the meeting was spent filling in gaps regarding contact person and size of gift for some of the prospects.

The greater part of the meeting was spent putting creative team energy into identifying even *more* prospects who might be approached. Many team members had not thought about their acquaintances' and contacts' own suggestions of who would be interested in the program. Still other team members had not thought previously about the certain other aspects of the program, and were now able to think of additional prospects who might have an interest.

By the end of the two hours, the master list grew from 150 names to well over 250 individuals, businesses, and foundations. Everyone was delighted that they had a significant list of donors and prospects with an identified interest in the new program. Team members also enjoyed the time together, since brainstorming creative ideas and watching their list grow was a lot of fun.

Summary

One of the best ways to involve all team members in fundraising is in identifying donors. This is an easy task that everyone can do, regardless of their squeamishness about cultivation, solicitation, and recognition. Basically, everyone knows someone who might make a contribution to your organization.

As you are identifying donors, think about contributors who are already making gifts to your organization. Might some current donors be asked for a repeat gift and major contribution? Are there lapsed donors who might have a special interest in a project that you need funded? Make sure you don't leave them out of your identification process.

Keep careful track of prospects and donors. Some nonprofits will have staff who are the database managers. Other groups will rely on volunteers, such as board members or nonboard volunteers with some skills in maintaining databases.

The following is a list of activities for team members for this important fundraising step of identifying donors.

Team in Action: Summary of Tasks

Everyone

- Identifies friends, colleagues, businesses, vendors, and so forth who may have an interest in learning more about your organization and making a donation.

- Participates in a work session to build prospect lists.

Leadership group

- Takes the lead in identifying donors, starting with the board chair and executive director.

- Organizes and attends, and one member facilitates, the work session for all team members to identify donors.

- Ensures the organization has an adequate tracking system for managing prospects and donors.

- Periodically evaluates the growth of prospect lists and the number who are becoming donors.

Remaining team members

- Regularly add names to the prospect lists, giving as much information as possible about the prospect to the list keepers.

- If there are staff doing data inputting and management about prospects and donors, volunteer to help wherever possible. If no staff are currently managing donor and prospect data, develop a task force to get this started.

- Research new foundation and corporation prospects. This may be done by an on-going task force (if the organization is large enough) or by a board member or nonboard volunteer who has research skills and is willing to do this task on a one-time basis.

- Research current donors to determine upgrade possibilities. This may be done by a small task force of staff (with a development director if you have this position), the board, or nonboard volunteers.

Chapter 9

Cultivating Donors with Good Communication

WHILE YOU IDENTIFY new prospects for your organization and donors who can give more significant gifts, your fundraising team should be cultivating them. *Cultivation* is the process of building relationships with prospects and donors. It is *all* of the strategies, plans, communications, events, and activities used to motivate an individual to make a donation. Therefore, cultivation is more than just education and involvement, though they are important steps in the process.

One of fundraising's basic maxims is "People give to people." What that means is that to a great extent, the cultivation process is all about nurturing personal relationships between people. One person alone, be it an executive director, a development director, a board member, or another volunteer, simply does not have enough hours in the workday to establish a personal relationship with every prospective and current donor. This is one of the most compelling reasons for team involvement. Simply put, the more people involved, the more people (read *potential donors)* reached.

You will soon see that some team members seem to know everybody in the corporate community and therefore are great at visiting potential company donors. Other team members are great at public speaking and can effectively present the agency's case for support to civic, church, social, and community groups. Cultivation can be both formal (communication via newsletters, case statement development, and presentations) and informal (donor visits, social gatherings). Here are several ideas for your team's efforts.

Cultivation Through Informal Means

Everyone on the team can participate in informing and communicating with others about a nonprofit's vital work. Countless opportunities await each of us every day—at the office, at social gatherings, the fitness center, and, yes, even at the bus stop. Telling others about your organization's work should be a joy if you are committed to the cause.

Informal education takes place any time, anywhere, any day. And all team members must be entrepreneurial by taking advantage of situations and opportunities when they can share information about their nonprofit agency with others. And this can happen almost anywhere—even in an informal car pool.

For example, Cheryl Clarke relates the story of a board member of a community arts organization who rides a commuter bus to work every day unless he happens to take advantage of an informal car pool. (An informal car pool is formed when an automobile driver picks up two or more people waiting at a bus stop. In the San Francisco Bay Area, informal carpooling is popular, as cars with three or more passengers can use the car pool lanes and get to work faster.)

In this particular informal car pool, the conversation turned to a discussion of the lack of adequate funding for the arts. Both the driver and other passenger shared an appreciation for the arts. The board member seized the moment. He described what his community arts organization was doing to support local visual and performing artists. Always prepared, he had copies of the agency's brochure in his briefcase, which he gave to each of his fellow commuters. By the end of the morning's commute, this board member had informed and educated two more people about his nonprofit and its work. Whether he knew it at the time or not, he had participated in one key step in the fundraising process—and all before 8 A.M.

Formal Cultivation Techniques

Cultivating prospects and donors more formally can take a variety of forms. Written communication can include newsletters, brochures, press releases, annual reports, and Web sites. There are also press conferences, public service announcements, and videos. For major donor prospects, your formal communication may consist of personal visits—not to ask for money, but to inform the potential donor of your work and to better understand their interests and commitment to your agency.

Delivering the right message at the right time by the right person to the right constituency is a challenge for nearly every organization. By effectively using your nonprofit's fundraising team, you can ensure that all of your external communications get the best results.

The ultimate result you are trying to achieve with formal cultivation is to raise funds for needed services. It's important to remember that communication through cultivation and fundraising functions are closely connected and interrelated. Individuals, foundations, and corporations will not financially support your agency unless they know about it. Therefore, it is critical that your fundraising team communicate clearly and often with your community.

Where to Start Formal Cultivation

Formally cultivating donors should start with having a good case statement. This three- to four-page document presents a "snapshot" of the nonprofit as it currently exists: its mission, programs, personnel, finances, and facts about the population you are serving. The case statement is extremely valuable because it gets everyone connected with the organization—board members, staff, and other nonboard volunteers—on the same page of the playbook. Having read a nonprofit's case statement, you would know all of the key facts about the organization, its programs, and how it meets constituent needs.

It is also valuable because it helps a nonprofit provide a clear message to the public about the organization—why it exists, who it serves, and what it needs to provide good quality services. Ensuring a clear and strong message is extremely important to successful fundraising.

A case statement is meant to be an internal document. That is, the case statement generally is not distributed to outside constituencies, rather it serves as a platform for preparing all fundraising-related materials, such as brochures, appeal letters, grant proposals, and planned giving materials.

Team Involvement in Preparing Case Statements

Because a case statement usually is an internal document, it often is written by team members who are most involved with the organization. If there is a development director in your organization, she or he will be involved with creating a case statement, and other team members will help draft it. An executive director might also take the lead in this activity. The draft should be distributed by its writers to everyone on the team for review and comments. This will help ensure that all team members feel they have had input to its development. Once completed, the writers of the case statement should distribute it to all members of the team for them to use as part of their informal and formal cultivation of prospects and donors.

What to do if . . . In cultivation, one of the most important responsibilities for the leadership team is the delivery of a consistent message. The leadership group should make certain that all the organization's communications, including the internal case statement, accurately reflect the core values and mission of the agency.

What happens if your message is confusing to current and prospective donors, as well as other constituencies? Cheryl Clarke relates an example in which the central mission of an arts education organization was getting lost amid the clutter surrounding its annual, hugely successful, street-painting festival. To many in the community, the festival itself was the main reason the organization existed. The agency's other year-round programs were not clearly highlighted.

At the urging of the agency's fundraising leadership, the board and staff evaluated the agency case statement and external communications materials for the festival. They concluded that their core mission—year-round arts programming—was not featured prominently enough in the external materials. They agreed that future cultivation efforts needed to deliver a better message about the agency's mission and programs. Today, festival visitors, as well as those who read and hear about it in the local media, are more likely to get the right message about the organization as an arts education agency with a wonderfully successful festival.

Each nonprofit agency has its own image, be it one of advocacy, compassionate care, musical or artistic excellence, or environmental stewardship. To achieve fundraising success, all communications about the agency must clearly reflect and support this image. I invite the fundraising team to ask: What is the public's image of our agency? Does the public's opinion reflect who we really are? And if not, how could our cultivation techniques better present the image we wish to convey? These are questions for the team to ask and then find the answers.

Involving Prospects and Donors

Studies routinely show that individuals are most likely to make their largest gifts to a nonprofit when they are involved with the agency. So in addition to communicating well with prospects and donors, one simple, never-ending goal for the entire fundraising team is always to seek new ways to get more and more people involved with the organization, its programs, and its fundraising activities.

The importance of having significant volunteer involvement is well illustrated by Cheryl Clarke in Chapter Seven in an example concerning a public library's pending capital campaign. From the very start of the pre-campaign planning phase, the library's fundraising leadership group encouraged participation of the Friends of the Library, a group mainly of seniors who assist the library's staff in book sorting, cataloging, and shelving, as well as managing the library's annual book sales. The Friends were invited to planning meetings involving architects, interior designers, and space planners, and were asked for their ideas about how to transform an antiquated historic building for use in the twenty-first century. They were also invited to a series of fundraising workshops to learn about the fundraising process and how the campaign would be structured. It wasn't surprising to learn that several of the campaign's leadership gifts were made by the Friends of the Library. It was almost inevitable.

Formal Cultivation—Team Activities

Looking first at team efforts to increase involvement, here are some strategies I have used.

The executive director could discuss with the nonprofit agency's program staff whether, and how, volunteers can help in the area of programs. Would volunteer docents enable a conservation group to initiate an outreach program for youth and teens? Can volunteers assist skilled, professional craftsmen in the restoration of a historic ship? Are additional volunteers needed to deliver hot meals to the homebound elderly?

In addition to helping in the program area, additional nonboard volunteers can also participate directly as members of the fundraising team. A development director may be able to enlist the help of a volunteer group, such as an auxiliary or "friends" group, to organize a fundraising event that will benefit the agency, such as a library's annual book sale. An animal welfare agency might have a core group of volunteers who organize a gigantic flea market for the organization. What is especially important is that nonboard fundraising efforts raise much-appreciated funds without taxing staff.

You might also be able to secure the involvement of service organizations if you have construction projects or if your building needs painting.

Team members can also get involved in communicating with prospects and donors. Often, several different techniques may be employed simultaneously, depending on the size of your team and your need to get your message out to prospects and donors. The following list is just the beginning of the communication techniques you may use to cultivate donors:

- Agency newsletter
- Organization brochures and other written materials
- Events
- Performances
- Parties

- Tours

- Social gatherings

- Personal conversations between fundraising team members and the potential donor

Given these possibilities, there's ample opportunity for *each* team member to participate in the cultivation step of the fundraising process. Because often several activities are happening at once, some organizations find it valuable to form cultivation task forces in which team members can participate. This helps to keep the flow of cultivation organized and the fundraising team members active and engaged.

Forming Cultivation Task Forces

It's important to have a good cultivation strategy so that team members don't find themselves tripping over one another as they do their tasks. This cultivation strategy becomes part of your overall fundraising plan as described in Chapter Six. The cultivation strategy also becomes the basis for putting together cultivation task forces. These small groups can help keep things on track and ensure communication among everyone participating in cultivation.

You may also want one staff member, such as the executive director or a development director, to have solo responsibility for some tasks such as cultivating major donors. Every organization will have a different plan to implement their strategy. The important point to remember is to structure the team to be as productive as possible.

To establish task forces, members of the leadership group should review the team surveys (described in Chapter Three) to begin identification of who is interested in cultivation activities. A list of who is interested in doing what and the special skills of team members can be developed prior to going to the full team. Often, you'll find that the people you have identified as being interested in cultivation serve as "cheerleaders" to draw more people to the task forces. So it is beneficial first to find out who they are and have some discussion with them about their interest in task forces and possibly taking a lead with one of them.

With team members' interests in mind, the leadership group can bring everyone together for some brainstorming and discussion on cultivation activities. Set some boundaries on this discussion or you may find yourselves with long lists of great ideas and not enough human or financial resources to implement them. The following set of questions can be used to help have a fruitful discussion that leads to putting your team into action with some good strategies.

WORKSHEET 9.1

Developing a Cultivation Strategy

1. What communication techniques have we used that have been particularly effective with our current donors?
2. What communication techniques have we seen used in other organizations that might also be effective with our donors?
3. Which of these techniques are possible for our organization to undertake?
4. How do we currently involve donors and prospects in our programs, events, and so forth.
5. What else might we do to involve people in our activities?

After your cultivation strategy is determined by the team, interested team members can form task forces to carry out the activities. These task forces may consist of two people or ten people, depending on the need and interest. When creating task forces, remember that there is much that the individual members of the fundraising team can do to implement the agency's ideas on communications and involvement. For example, team members can serve as effective spokespersons on behalf of the organization. Although the executive director typically serves as the agency's "official" spokesperson, board members and other volunteers can be trained also to serve in this role, thereby significantly expanding the agency's reach into the community. Volunteer spokespersons can address civic and community groups, such as Rotary Clubs, alumni organizations, and church groups. Through their efforts, they can tell hundreds, perhaps even thousands, of people about the agency, its mission, vision, and programs.

Other team members may be excellent wordsmiths and can assist the nonprofit on a task force that contributes articles to the newsletter, writes brochure copy, or prepares press releases. Still others may have contacts with the local media and can help the agency pitch stories for placement with newspapers, magazines, television, and radio stations. And there may be a task force specifically charged with watching legislative actions that could have an impact on your organization. Members of this task force would carry the nonprofit's message to politicians and bring back information to the team about pending legislation.

Each task force will need a leader who makes sure that everyone stays on track and that activities are completed according to the plan. In larger organizations, communications task forces are likely to be led by a director of public relations or a chief communications officer and may consist of writers, editors, and graphics designers who are on staff or are volunteers. In these larger nonprofit agencies, it is important for members of the fundraising team, particularly the executive director and development director, to work closely with the task forces to make sure that external communications support the agency's fundraising efforts. The executive director should communicate that this is both an expectation and a priority.

Cultivation task forces should be encouraged to hold regular joint meetings to share ideas and plans, and to work together to build communications strategies for areas of overlap. At the beginning of the nonprofit's fiscal year, everyone should provide each other with their respective task force's upcoming calendar of events and action plan.

Medium-sized and smaller organizations are not likely to have a full-time staff person, and certainly not an entire department, handling its public relations, communications functions, or fund development. In these organizations, board members, nonboard volunteers, and staff with requisite skills may provide the leadership needed for the cultivation task forces.

Although task forces are important if you want to reach a wide audience in many ways, it is also crucial to realize that the leadership of the organization must have some overall responsibility in cultivating donors. Given their positions, the executive director and board chairperson will be intimately involved in cultivating the nonprofit's major donor prospects. If there is a development director, this person may facilitate the entire cultivation process by helping set up task forces and staying in touch with their progress. In agencies with no development director, some other leadership group member (or members) oversees the task forces.

Regardless of who is actually responsible for external communications, the goal is make certain that these efforts support the nonprofit's fundraising efforts by taking advantage of public relations opportunities when they arise.

The worksheet below will help you start your process for setting up cultivation task forces. Use it to determine the best cultivation activities for the year and what task forces are needed.

WORKSHEET 9.2

Developing Cultivation Task Forces

1. What cultivation activities have we identified for this year?

2. Do these activities correspond with the new prospects we have identified for cultivation? Yes or No? If no, what additional cultivation activities should we be doing to reach these new prospects?

    - _____
    - _____
    - _____
    - _____

3. Do the team surveys indicate sufficient interest in cultivation to carry out the activities we have listed? Yes or No? If no, prioritize the cultivation activities above and list only those with the highest priority.

    - _____
    - _____
    - _____
    - _____

4. What are the task forces needed to carry out these cultivation activities?

    - _____
    - _____
    - _____
    - _____

5. Based on the team surveys, who might be a good task leader and member for these task forces?

Task Force 1	Task Force 2	Task Force 3	Task Force 4
1.	1.	1.	1.
2.	2.	2.	2.
3.	3.	3.	3.
4.	4.	4.	4.

After the leadership group has completed the worksheet, it is, of course, essential to check with those people you have identified as potential task force members to see whether they have the interest and time.

Example of Cultivation—The Team in Action

In Chapter Four, I introduced an environmental organization that successfully organized itself into a fundraising team. One of the steps the board, staff, and nonboard volunteers took was to form cultivation task forces. Ideas for task forces were initially conceived by a very creative board member who served as chair of the fundraising committee. He knew that many board members were very reluctant to do any type of fundraising, including cultivation, so he generated a list of twelve possible task forces with humorous titles and a very clear description of what each task force was expected to do. When he presented his list to the board and staff, they enjoyed the humor and were able to have a good discussion about what task forces they thought would be most valuable for the organization; each board and staff member signed up for at least one group. The fundraising chair was also able to get volunteer leaders for each task force from among the board membership.

After the meeting, the fundraising chairperson was applauded by everyone for helping bring the fundraising team more solidly together via humor and gentle persuasion to motivate everyone to get involved.

Summary

By communicating often with prospects and donors, and by getting people involved, your organization will not only benefit from the additional hands that allow more work to be done, but also because those individuals are apt to respond very generously when asked for financial support.

Your fundraising team can work together to design the most effective, efficient cultivation strategy for donors to obtain whatever resources (time, money, and people) are needed to raise the most contributed funds. A development director, if there is one, will often take the lead in this activity; otherwise, someone in the organization with good public relations and marketing skills should take the lead.

The list below summarizes many of the tasks I have described that lead to successful cultivation. Use it as a guide to help create your best strategy for your own organization.

Team in Action: Summary of Tasks

Everyone

- Informally talk about your organization with anyone you can think of to educate them about your work and gain their interest and involvement.
- Participate in brainstorming of formal cultivation techniques.
- Understand the mission of your organization and how everyone wants it to be perceived in your community.
- Attend cultivation events or other activities to spread the word about your organization.

Leadership group

- Review team member surveys to match individuals to possible cultivation activities. Compare fundraising plan activities to member interest.

- Organize a brainstorming session to develop the cultivation activities. (This may be part of developing your fundraising plan.)
- Draft a cultivation strategy that effectively gets your message out to the community. (This may be done by an executive director, development director, or board member with public relations skills, and is given to the whole team for discussion and approval.)
- Help interested board, staff, and nonboard volunteers organize into task forces to carry out the decided upon cultivation activities.
- Monitor the progress of task forces. Have frequent meetings with task force leaders (who may or may not be part of the leadership group) to understand how work is progressing. Be involved with finding solutions to problems.
- Join task forces that are of interest to you.
- Manage sensitive cultivation issues, such as a particular effort to communicate to major donors that requires the board chair or executive director's involvement.
- Oversee all final development of written communication materials.
- Ensure a consistent and clear message for your organization.
- Make sure that all external communications support the fundraising activities.
- Motivate, encourage, and celebrate small wins with your fellow team members.

Interested board, staff, and nonboard volunteers

- Join a cultivation task force that matches your skills and interests.
- Help determine the best ways for your task force to complete your designated activity, and participate fully in its implementation.
- Develop benchmarks for your task force in order to allow yourselves some small wins to celebrate.
- Communicate often with other team members working on cultivation strategies to ensure consistency and a clear message to prospects and donors.

Chapter 10

Asking for a Gift

EVENTUALLY, SOMEBODY, SOMEWHERE, somehow must ask someone for some money. All your cultivation efforts won't amount to a pile of pennies unless you ask your prospects for a contribution.

Asking your donors and prospects for contributions requires that you determine the appropriate vehicle to use in a given solicitation (that is, letter, e-mail, phone call, or face-to-face meeting). The overarching question is, How can a nonprofit efficiently and effectively reach as many likely prospects and donors as possible? Shaping the decision are the all-important considerations of time, personnel, and money. Methods such as direct mail, telemarketing, and Internet marketing are good ways to solicit large numbers of small donors, whereas personal letters, personal phone calls, and face-to-face visits are ways to solicit larger gifts.

If your organization has a development director, this person (and his or her professional staff, if yours is more than a one-person shop) takes the lead for the team for implementing the solicitation techniques that are designed to reach lots of people and likely to generate small gifts. Such programs usually employ techniques such as direct (or mass) mail, telemarketing, and Internet marketing. Organizations can rely on the professional knowledge and experience of a development director to make these kinds of programs successful.

Although development directors may have overall accountability and responsibility for these fundraising tasks, there is still a place for assistance from team members. Nonboard volunteers are especially good at getting the mass mailing out the door and in making phone calls to ask for contributions. Board members can also be valuable team players in making phone requests.

Other donor prospects will require a more individualized form of asking, and you will find some team members that have expertise and an interest in making more personal solicitations. Board members, staff members, and nonboard volunteers can write personal notes on appeal letters addressed to their friends and acquaintances. They can make personal telephone calls. They can host, attend, and sell tickets to fundraising events. They can participate in walk-a-thons, dance marathons, and pet walks. They can personally visit prospects to ask for support.

If your nonprofit does not have a development director to lead the process of securing gifts, don't despair. This is an opportunity for one or more team members interested in solicitations to take the lead. Read on for ideas on forming solicitation task forces to secure contributions for an organization that may or may not have a development director.

Organizing the Team for Solicitations

The leadership group manages this process, and if there is a development director, this position will have much to do. Without a development director, the leadership group will need to divide up the management, or someone with skills similar to a development director's will need to take the lead. This means handling many of the behind-the-scenes logistics to make sure the team members have everything they need to be successful in making personal solicitations. For example, someone must make sure that appeal letters are received by team members, who will then personally pen notes to friends and colleagues. Other tasks include scheduling meetings, providing team members with researched prospect information, and preparing regular reports that track progress. If you are using task forces for solicitation, it means making sure these small groups have what they need to get their job done.

If yours is an organization that will be handling numerous types of solicitation in a year, you may want to organize your team into task forces similar to cultivation task forces, described in the previous chapter. For instance, let's say your fundraising plan indicates that there will be an annual event, two prospect mailings to the list you are developing plus a mailing to current donors, a major donor campaign, and ongoing grantwriting to foundations. Using the task force concept, you would set up four of them; organizationally, it would look like Figure 10.1.

Interested team members would sign up for the task force that appeals to them. The leadership group may want to develop brief descriptions of each task force's responsibilities, based on the objectives identified in the

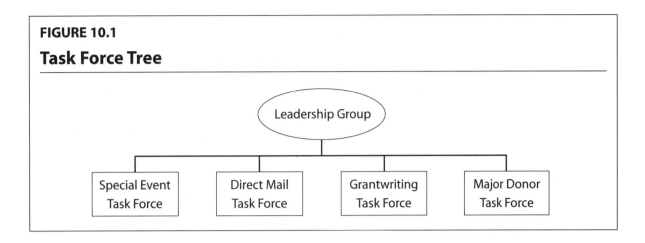

FIGURE 10.1

Task Force Tree

fundraising plan. For instance, the Direct Mail Task Force's job might be described as follows.

Direct Mail Task Force

Annual Objectives (taken from fundraising plan):

1. *Maintain or exceed a 70 percent renewal rate from current donors.*

2. *Upgrade a minimum of 15 percent of donors to the next giving level.*

3. *Increase the donor base by a minimum of 25 percent.*

Responsibilities:

1. *Ensure that all direct mail solicitations of the xyz organization are accurate, timely, and reflect the image we wish to project to our prospects and donors.*

2. *Develop appealing letters and package pieces that will motivate prospects to give generously.*

3. *Manage designers, mailing houses, and list brokers involved in direct mail solicitations.*

4. *Conduct at least two prospect mailings and one donor renewal mailing while staying within budget.*

What to do if . . . What if team members are not interested in asking for contributions? I acknowledge that actually asking a person for money is not easy for many reasons. Many people are afraid of being rejected. Many others are uncomfortable because they don't know how to ask. Fear and uncertainly can be diminished, if not completely eliminated, through education and training. It is important for individuals to understand that people will say "no" to a request for several valid reasons, and rarely are they personal to the solicitor. "No" may mean "I'm broke," "Not now," "You asked for too much money," or "This cause is not a high enough priority." Your team training should be designed to help board members, staff, and nonboard volunteers overcome their fears and demystify the whole fundraising process.

Even with education and training, not everyone on the team will be able to do it—or do it well. That's OK so long as these folks are involved in at least one, and preferably more, of the other fundraising steps. It may be easier for some team members to write notes rather than make personal visits. Others may enjoy the thrill of sitting down with a prospect and asking for a big gift. You may have a group of nonboard volunteers who love to organize fundraising events and another group who are ready, willing, and able to make telephone calls on the organization's behalf. The challenge is making sure that each person on the fundraising team is doing the job most suited to him or her.

Generally speaking, program and support staff are not usually engaged in direct asking for donations because it may appear they are trying to raise funds for their salaries. However, staff who are interested in doing solicitations can be valuable additions to a duo or trio of volunteers who are making personal solicitations because staff can answer the more difficult program-related questions.

Under a team-based fundraising approach, the key concept is that asking for money cannot be the sole responsibility of one or two people within the nonprofit. This task cannot be charged to the development director or executive director "to see what she (or they) can do." Securing a nonprofit's future, which thereby allows it to continue to offer programs that address a societal need, is a bigger job than any one person can possibly manage. It requires hands-on, labor-intensive participation from everyone.

Team Accountability in Solicitations

Team accountability for fulfilling these tasks can sometimes be complicated. It takes strong leadership, specifically from the board chairperson, to ensure that a fellow board member makes the appointment with a prospective donor or that a volunteer sells her ten tickets to the annual fundraiser. First, the board chair must be involved. He or she must also meet with prospects and sell tickets to the fundraising event.

Second, accountability is best made to a peer. In other words, board members should be accountable to board members, nonboard volunteers should be accountable to other volunteers, and staff should be accountable to other staff. Because the board of directors supervises her performance and is therefore her boss, an executive director will find it awkward at best, and impossible at worst, to hold a board member accountable for failing to write personal notes on twenty-five annual appeal letters. Therefore, I recommend that she never be put in this position. Similarly, an executive director, dean, or chief executive officer of a nonprofit agency should not solicit board members. This is a job for a board peer—be it the board chair or the chair of the development committee.

Example—Team Asking in Action

A San Francisco Bay Area animal welfare organization decided several years ago to have a spring extravaganza that included a fundraising "petwalk." This petwalk was modeled on the traditional walk-a-thons except that individuals were encouraged to bring their pets with them. Most traditional walk-a-thons discourage you from including your pet. This organization planned their event around having lots of dogs walking along with their human companions. As a side note, in the first year of the petwalk, advertising did not focus on bringing just *dogs* for the walk, and this resulted in people showing up with cats, birds, and iguanas. Fortunately, the world's largest animal free-for-all did not happen. But the organization did learn to be specific about what pets are appropriate for this type of event.

As the development director of that organization, I had the job of organizing a sizeable task force of staff, board members, and nonboard volunteers to make the petwalk a success. A couple members of the task force took responsibility for sending out pledge forms and tracking those who signed up and sent in their pledges. Several others managed the logistics of the walk, including making sure there was water along the route for humans and pets, good signage and walk monitors so we didn't have lost people and their pets, and food for everyone at the end of the walk. The executive director and a board member, as task force members, worked with us and with the public relations department to advertise the whole spring extravaganza, including the petwalk.

The task force made sure that on the day of the event there were staff from the clinic and the animal behavior department on hand to manage any emergencies. Other staff and many nonboard volunteers in the organization showed their team spirit for the event as walk monitors, water pourers, and food distributors. Board members signed up for the walk and gathered pledges from friends and work colleagues. By the day of the event, almost everyone who did not have to work at the organization was out making sure the first annual petwalk was a howling success. And because it was a team effort, the event was successful beyond our wildest imaginations. Petwalk happened annually for several years thereafter, still organized by a task force and with a strong team effort to make it happen.

Summary

Team members can be involved in solicitation in a variety of ways, from acquiring small gifts through direct mail to obtaining large grants and individual donations. Solicitation might include writing a brief note on a letter that is being mailed to a colleague of a team member. It might also include sitting down with a prospective major donor and asking for a large gift. Team members can and should select solicitation activities with which they feel most comfortable.

In some organizations, where several solicitation activities will be conducted in a year, it might be practical to form task forces. These small groups (consisting of anywhere from two or more people) can organize and implement solicitations and take responsibility for them. Overall responsibility for soliciting contributions falls on the leadership group who monitors and assists task forces or individuals who are doing solicitations.

Team in Action: Summary of Activities

Everyone

- Identify a solicitation activity that you would enjoy working on and let the leadership group know of your interest.

- Attend special events and other fundraising activities.

Leadership group

- Establish solicitation task forces if that seems most appropriate for your organization.

- Determine the key individual on the leadership group to give support to the solicitation process and manage all the activities.

- Decide whether there are any donors or prospects who need very special attention by a particular individual at the organization. Make sure that these donors and prospects are well served.

- Monitor the overall solicitation effort to ensure success.

Chapter 11

Saying Thank You and Providing Stewardship

AFTER RECEIVING A GIFT, especially a large one, there's a tendency among many organizations to move on to the next major gift solicitation and forget that there's more to be done with the current donor. The remaining work, of course, is thanking the donor, acknowledging his or her generosity through appropriate donor recognition, and finally, ensuring good stewardship for donors.

It is critical that donors—all donors—be thanked for their support of your agency. The value of thoughtful recognition and stewardship cannot, and should not, be overlooked by a nonprofit agency. And the importance of involving the full fundraising team in the process should not be ignored.

Saying Thanks

In reading this chapter, keep the following key fundraising maxim in mind: *It's almost impossible to thank a donor too much.* In most circumstances, people want to be thanked and recognized for their generosity. This means that your fundraising team must be prepared to deliver a personal thank you and, in many cases, also prepare a public acknowledgment. On occasion, you will find an individual who, for whatever reason, prefers anonymity, which of course should be respected and granted.

There are many opportunities to thank and acknowledge your donors, and to get the fundraising team involved in the process. The first opportunity arises when the donation arrives. Nonprofits should have an internal system and process for promptly recording and acknowledging all gifts—whether large or small. A member of your leadership group with strong technological skills can take a leadership role in establishing and managing this system.

Someone else on the fundraising team can inform team members about new donations that result from their cultivation and solicitation. If there is a development director, this person often coordinates this activity for the entire team.

Let's run through a typical scenario following the arrival of a major gift. When a large donation arrives at your agency, typically in the form of a check, the person managing acknowledgments should be informed immediately by whomever processes the agency's checks. For major gifts, the executive director should also be immediately informed. I recommend that your executive director—and all executive directors—promptly telephone each major donor to let him or her know that the gift arrived and to say "thanks" formally on behalf of the agency. (Once again, it bears repeating that each agency defines for itself what constitutes a "major gift." For some organizations, it is $100, while for others it may be $5,000.) Such a phone call provides the executive director with an opportunity to remind the donor of how his or her gift will be used by the agency and what impact it will have on the work being done. Making this phone call is not only good recognition, but also good stewardship, as discussed later.

You may ask, How can an overworked executive director fit one more thing into already busy days? I can tell you that even the busiest ones do. When it comes to building relationships with donors, especially major donors, it is imperative that executive directors make the time. I've worked with many executive directors, and all have their own style. Some are more spontaneous and will immediately pick up the phone to thank a donor for a gift. Others keep to their calendar and will schedule a set time(s) during the week to make these calls. Regardless of the method used, these executive directors enjoy making these calls. For the majority of executive directors I know, talking to individuals who care enough about an agency and its work to write a substantial check is pure joy.

But this joyful experience need not be limited to just the executive director. Calling and thanking major donors can be a shared responsibility among all the members of the fundraising team. When a large gift arrives, the team member in charge of managing the gift recognition process should notify each team member who played a major role in securing the donation. It may be appropriate, depending on the relationships between the donor and individual team members, for one or more team members to also telephone or write to the donor and say "thanks."

The following chart will help your team keep track of incoming major donations and the important thank-you process.

WORKSHEET 11.1						
Major Donor Acknowledgments						
Major Donor Name/Phone Number	**Amount of Gift/ Date Received**	**Purpose of Gift**	**Person(s) Soliciting Gift**	**Person Recognizing Gift**	**Date of Call**	**Comments**

Remember that providing timely notification to team members about the major gifts is a courtesy. It can also prevent embarrassment, as the following case study contributed by Cheryl Clarke illustrates.

An attorney who served on the board of directors for his law school had been actively involved in the cultivation of one of his classmates and professional peers. The two men frequently saw each other at social and at work-related and alumni functions. For years, the board member had been urging his colleague to make a larger financial commitment to their alma mater. The board member's friend eventually did so; however, no one from the law school notified this board member when the gift came in. The men continued to see each other at various meetings and social functions. After a few months passed, the donor, clearly perturbed, said to the board member, "Gee, for the past year or so, you couldn't say enough positive things about our old school. So I make a $1,000 gift and you can't even say 'thanks'?"

Oops. The development office at the law school had dropped the ball, or in this case, the gift. When the check came in, the development director should have immediately notified the board member who had been cultivating the prospective donor. Because of a bump in the communications process between agency staff and volunteers, a dedicated board member was embarrassed. Furthermore, a new major donor, one that had been diligently recruited, felt unacknowledged by his colleague and peer.

Providing Written Acknowledgment

Telephoned "thank yous"—whether from an executive director, a board member, or other nonboard volunteer—definitely do not replace an agency-prepared formal written acknowledgment mailed to a donor. It is a frequently cited rule within the nonprofit field that all gifts from all donors (no matter what size of gift) should be acknowledged in writing within forty-eight hours of receipt. This is certainly a good standard toward which to aspire.

For some organizations, especially those with large development staffs, it may be routine practice to process gifts and prepare written acknowledgments within two business days. For others, particularly grassroots agencies that have no staff, it may be more realistic to expect such turnaround within a week.

But the objective is simple: Be as prompt as you can in letting donors know that you have received their gifts. I am fairly confident that most donors are a lot like us. When we make our own personal contributions, large or small, we appreciate promptly hearing from the agency that our money was received and is appreciated.

There's another reason for providing donors with a written acknowledgment: The law requires it for large gifts. At press time, Internal Revenue Service regulations state "that donors must obtain receipts for gifts of $250 or more if they plan to take a tax deduction for the gift."

Team Involvement in Recognizing Gifts

As discussed above, it is critical to acknowledge gifts as soon as possible after they are received. However, this should be just the beginning of a well-conceived program for acknowledging and recognizing donors that is orchestrated by the entire fundraising team.

Throughout the year, nonprofit organizations must continue to say "thanks" to their supporters, and many have come up with some pretty creative ways of doing so. The best integrate the fundraising team in this process. Here are some ideas that have worked in organizations we know.

Thankathon

Agencies with several fundraising team members should consider holding a thankathon. A thankathon is similar to the phonathon, but instead of asking board members and nonboard volunteers to call and ask for money, they call donors to say "thanks." That's it, just "thanks." No pitch. No solicitation. No opportunity for rejection.

In organizations that have held a thankathon, two things occur. The first is that the response by participant callers is overwhelmingly enthusiastic and positive. The second is that this activity provides an opportunity for all members of the fundraising team to learn to work together—and to enjoy it!

Using a thankathon as an early project for your fundraising team may be the best possible ice breaker for the group, and one that is fairly failproof. (It is impossible for someone to hang up or object when he or she is being thanked.) A thankathon can be organized by either the team's leadership group as a whole or by a committee or task force comprising other team members. It may be a good idea to have staff members (certainly the development director, if your agency has one, and perhaps program staff as well), board members, and nonboard volunteers all participate in making the calls to bring everyone into the process.

Small grassroots organizations may find that they can realistically reach all of their supporters in one or two nights. For these organizations, a thankathon provides a unique opportunity for fundraising team members to personally connect with everyone who cares about, and supports, the organization. Medium-sized and larger nonprofits may find it unrealistic to telephone every donor, and may instead elect to call a certain segment of donors; for example, those who give above a specific gift level.

Holding a successful thankathon requires the following ingredients: an identified donor population, enthusiastic callers, telephones, and a sense of fun. Unlike a telemarketing campaign or phonathon, very little needs to be scripted and rehearsed. Callers can be more spontaneous. And other than saying "thanks," they may want to tell donors some specifics about how their money was used, or will be used, by the agency in responding to an urgent community need.

Worksheet 11.1, developed for major donor acknowledgment, can also be very effective for thankathon calls.

In conclusion, you should consider including a thankathon in your agency's team-based fundraising plan for two reasons. First, a thankathon lets donors know that you care about them during the year—not just when your agency needs money. Second, it's a proven, wonderful way to get fearful, shy, or otherwise reticent team members talking to donors—and actually enjoying it. From this stage, it is not such a large step to get the members of your fundraising team to start asking for donations.

Appreciation Events

Unlike fundraising events, where the objective is to raise money, appreciation events are held simply to acknowledge and recognize donors. If an image of rubber chicken dinners, gold plaques, and long speeches comes to mind, think again! The best appreciation events are creative, innovative, fun, even quirky affairs.

Cheryl Clarke relates one of the more unusual appreciation events, which is an annual seal and sea lion release. Each year, major donors ($1,000 and above) to a wildlife rehab center get an opportunity to witness the release back to nature of formerly sick and injured seals and sea lions that have been rehabilitated back to health. Just after daybreak, donors board a chartered bus to travel to a remote beach location. (Releases are generally not public so as to limit crowd size and thus help possibly tentative and frightened animals have a better chance of quickly readjusting to life in the wild.) Other than renting a bus, the nonprofit's only other expense is providing donors a thermos or two of coffee and some sweet rolls.

This appreciation activity works not only because it is so unique, but also because members of the fundraising team also participate. Generally, the executive director, several board members, the development director, other staff members, and nonboard volunteers attend the release along with the major donors. It's pretty easy to build personal relationships between agency representatives and major donors when sharing the moment that a now-healthy seal plunges back into the ocean after months of rehabilitation.

Not every nonprofit can provide their major donors with the kind of spine-tingling experience described above. However, you can help make your organization's appreciation events successful by effectively using your fundraising team. Have the team's leadership group or a task force brainstorm ideas for appreciation events. Ask team members to host an event personally, such as a small cocktail party or a buffet dinner. And above all, encourage team members to attend such events—their very presence speaks volumes about their commitment and dedication to the organization.

Stewarding the Donor Relationship

Stewardship is all about spending your donors' gifts wisely and in accordance with donor wishes. It is also about continued relationship building with your donors and viewing them as the investors in your organization. *Stewarding a donor relationship* refers to all of the strategies and activities that a nonprofit organization employs to keep a current donor informed, involved, and motivated to give again.

A basic fundraising maxim holds that a nonprofit's best future prospects are its current donors. Therefore, stewardship is a year-round process of cultivating current donors for their next gifts. And like each of the other steps in successful fund development, effective stewardship requires the input, enthusiasm, skills, and talents of everyone on the fundraising team.

The Fundraising Team as Stewards

The leadership group serves as custodians for donor contributions. They, along with the full board of directors, have a moral, if not legal, obligation to make certain that the agency spends contributed funds as directed by the donors. In other words, if a written appeal asks for funds so the agency can purchase a certain piece of equipment, the contributions generated from that appeal should be used for that purpose and should not be redirected toward some other need, no matter how worthy.

Staff can make certain that controls are in place to prevent funds from being used for other than their restricted purpose. Everyone on the team should have a strong interest in making sure money raised is appropriately spent, since the likely outcome of breaching a donor's trust will mean that that trust will be difficult to win back, and donations will stop coming.

However, all responsibility does not rest with the staff. The board of directors ultimately has legal responsibility for the agency. The board should provide vigilant oversight. In some cases, they may need to demonstrate self-restraint in the face of financial instability and program and employee cutbacks. What board wouldn't be tempted to "temporarily" transfer funds from a restricted account to make payroll, especially if money from an annual appeal was expected any day? In recent years, more than one nonprofit has endured their donors' wrath as well as public humiliation for succumbing to such temptations. I encourage the whole fundraising team to remain vigilant in being good stewards of donor gifts.

Viewing Donors as Investors

One of the most frequent criticisms donors have about nonprofit agencies concerns communication, or rather the lack of it. "I only hear from the XYZ agency when they want to ask me for money!" is what some frustrated, and occasionally angry, donors say. In contrast, what nonprofit organizations want to hear donors say is, "I feel I am an investor in your organization and want to know more about what's going on—please tell me!" Part of good stewardship is helping donors understand that their investment in your nonprofit is making a difference in a way that is valued by the donor. The bottom line is that donors want to feel their values are respected and important to an organization, and that their gift is a good investment.

The fundraising team can be very active in helping donors understand they are valued and their gifts are making a difference. All the cultivation activities discussed in Chapter Nine are part of this side of good stewardship. Here are a few additional ways to involve the team in stewarding your donors.

Lectures by outside experts or experts on your organization's staff, workshops, and annual donor meetings are other ways that a nonprofit can keep in touch with its donors during the year and provide them with information.

Hosting lectures, workshops, and meetings requires an organization to commit both personnel and financial resources. Therefore, members of the fundraising team need to recognize the value of such efforts and make certain that these are included in the annual fundraising plan.

Interested fundraising team members can lend a hand in helping staff organize lectures, workshops, and meetings. Although these activities are not directly part of the fundraising process, they complement fund development by making donors and potential donors more aware of problems and issues in the community that your nonprofit addresses through its programs.

Like cultivation and donor recognition events, team members should also attend stewardship functions. Such occasions provide members of the team with natural opportunities to meet and mingle with the organization's donors. Remember, it is much easier for volunteer solicitors to ask others for money when they have already developed comfortable, familiar relationships with the prospects.

Getting Information

Although preceding sections focus on stewardship activities as a means for delivering information about the organization to donors, good stewardship isn't limited to agencies *talking* to donors. It also involves *listening* to what donors have to say. Therefore, the best stewardship strategies provide donors with a means to communicate with the agency. And by using a team-based approach to fundraising, a nonprofit organization will have more ears to hear what donors are saying.

Readership surveys, questionnaires, annual meetings, focus groups, and face-to-face meetings all provide a means for eliciting ideas, suggestions, and concerns from current donors. Organizations that establish a dialogue between donors and the nonprofit (as represented by the fundraising team) not only build stronger personal relationships, but also succeed at fundraising.

Example of Stewardship and Recognition

A San Francisco Bay Area organization was struggling to find a meaningful, and relatively inexpensive, way of recognizing their major donors (gifts over $100). Most of their donors had little interest in big, extravagant parties where lots of people gathered, and the donors did not want a lot of lavish attention for their generosity. Still, the nonprofit wanted to recognize the involvement and kindness of the donors. The nonprofit decided to host a series of intimate house parties as a recognition strategy. They decided that each house party would be more than a thank you; it would also be a stewardship event where donors would be told how their contributions had been used in the past year and where next year's priorities would be discussed for donor input (and buy-in).

Since the nonprofit is regionwide, it was felt that one house party in each county (of a nine-county area) would be the goal. The host of the house party would be the homeowner, although the nonprofit would cover expenses and help with logistics. It was estimated that each party would draw between thirty and forty-five people.

The leadership group began approaching board members and nonboard volunteers to offer their homes for the intimate recognition events, and the response was overwhelming. Board members and nonboard volunteers felt honored as team members to be asked to open up their homes for the parties. The only criteria used for selection was that the home could easily hold up to forty-five people and that it be centrally located in the county.

When the homes were selected for the parties, additional board members, staff, and nonboard volunteers formed "party logistics" task forces for each county to ensure that each party was a success.

Of course the parties were a success because of the involvement of so many people. Major donors said they had never been treated so royally, even though the costs were minimal. They also greatly appreciated the emphasis on giving them information on their contributions and how they helped advance the mission of the organization. The hosts thoroughly enjoyed having a party for which they had ready-made help to make it happen. And the task forces had a lot of fun planning and organizing each house party.

Summary

Every donor deserves some recognition, regardless of the size of the gift. Recognition should follow soon after the gift is received. Good stewardship means setting and holding high professional standards, communicating honestly with donors, and routinely seeking their wisdom, opinions, and concerns. The fundraising team must keep this in mind while busily raising funds in a highly competitive environment for donor dollars.

Team in Action: Summary of Activities

Everyone

- Complements the agency's formal acknowledgment process by personally thanking personal friends and colleagues for their donations

- Participates in stewardship activities, seeking opportunities to meet the agency's donors and develop relationships with them

Leadership group

- Participates in the agency's formal acknowledgment process by signing acknowledgment letters and making telephone calls to thank donors, particularly major donors

- Plans a stewardship program for the agency; strives to create an environment that fosters stewardship of all individuals who contribute to the success of the agency

- Designs and implements the agency's formal acknowledgment process; encourages board members and volunteers to thank their personal friends and colleagues for donations

Part Four

Charting Your Progress as a Team

Chapter 12

Evaluating the Progress and Health of Your Team

A KEY STEP in using a team approach to fundraising is evaluating the progress, effectiveness, and health of your fundraising team. This section looks at evaluation in terms of process *(How well did we do?)* and outcomes *(Did we have a positive impact on our organization and the community?)*. I demonstrate ways to evaluate team performance to help you look at the overall effectiveness of your team. Remember: Monitoring performance provides accountability to the team and inspires confidence as success is achieved. Part of this chapter is also devoted to measuring the health of your team. Because a team will have difficulty achieving its goals if it is not in good health, it is important to review and take notice of how well everyone is working together.

Nonprofits that take the time to plan their fundraising activities carefully and strategically can easily measure how well they are doing in reaching their fundraising goals and objectives. Good evaluation allows for midcourse corrections when the energy of team members is being drained because activities are not working well. Reports of successful fundraising activities can quickly energize team members and inspire others to work in or volunteer for the organization, as well as inspire community members to support such a successful group.

Developing a Team-Oriented Evaluation Process

As the leadership group is finalizing the fundraising team's goals and objectives with the other team members, careful thought needs to be given to evaluating success. It is imperative to discuss early-on what key evaluative questions you want answered and how you will measure whether the process is working. Specifically, the fundraising team needs to decide

1. What is success?

2. How do we measure this success?

3. What are the data sources and collection procedures, and who does the collection?

4. What is the frequency of evaluation?

5. What baseline are we using?

6. What reporting processes will keep the team informed?

The first crucial step in this process is for the team to discuss and reach consensus on what constitutes success. How will you know if the team has been successful—if the objectives are reached or new programs are started due to increased revenues, or by some other indicator? Each organization will have different ideas on what success means, and these ideas should be communicated throughout the team so everyone knows the standards.

One effective way of having this discussion is to bring everyone together as the fundraising plan is being finalized. Use part of this session to review and approve the plan, and another part of the session to determine how you know you have been successful in implementing the plan. This latter discussion allows for two things to happen: It helps team members understand that they are accountable for being successful, and it allows full team input into defining success.

You will probably find your team members eager to offer suggestions on standards of success, types of data to be collected, and the overall questions that your evaluation process needs to answer. As is true with planning processes, the more the team has input, the greater the buy-in to reaching a high level of success.

Determine What to Measure

Following the discussion on what success means, the leadership group should begin discussions with team members to decide on the key questions that should be answered. These questions should include process-related questions (*Did we do all that we said we were going to do this year?*) and outcome-related questions (*Did our fundraising have a positive impact on the growth of our organization?*).

Following is a list of questions you may want to use as a guide to developing your own set. It is important to develop questions that tie closely to the goals, objectives, and activities of your fundraising plan so that your questions are answerable through the fundraising activities you are conducting. Here are some suggested questions:

- Did the team meet the revenue-generating objectives for the year?

- Were the nonrevenue-generating objectives met for the year?

- Were objectives accomplished within the allocated fundraising budget for the year?

- What impact did our fundraising efforts have on the organization? On our target population?

The person in the leadership group with the most experience with evaluation would be the natural choice for developing a draft set of questions for the group and subsequently the whole team to view and discuss. When the set of questions is finalized, it is time to figure out how to answer them.

Data Sources and Collection

Leadership group members and other team members with experience in evaluation should discuss and determine what data sources to use to answer the key questions and how to collect that data.

You may decide that concentrating on collecting quantitative data is most efficient for you. These data are usually in the form of statistics that help an organization count, compare, and contrast. For example, you might collect data on all contributions from every fundraising method used, and compare and contrast this amount with results of previous years. There are other measures, such as

- The growth in numbers and types of donors

- The number of repeat donors

- The average gift size by type of donor

- The number of new donor markets

- The number of new clients served

- The percentage growth of agency programs

Numerous measurements can be made with quantitative data when such data are available. Team members can use these data to evaluate the effectiveness of both the fundraising process and its outcomes.

Qualitative data, however, provide descriptive information that is collected directly from those involved with fundraising or from your donors. You will be collecting qualitative data when you determine the team's effectiveness in working together (discussed later in this chapter). You may also want to gather this type of data to better understand the impact of your fundraising efforts.

Your donors are excellent sources of information on the quality of your fundraising program. Phone calls or surveys to donors to ask them whether the solicitations they receive are professional, well-timed, and compelling gives you important feedback. You may also want to find out their impressions of your programs and their reasons for choosing your organization for their gifts.

The community around you is also an important source of qualitative information about your fundraising. As part of the evaluation of your external communications, you may want to determine the community's perceptions of your organization and the need for your services. You may also want to explore their views on the quality of the materials they receive—especially if you send your newsletter or other publications to a broader base than your donor list.

Finally, your own objective review of the materials your organization produces is a good source of information on the quality of your fundraising program. Your solicitation materials can provide good feedback on possible changes that will make them more effective. Looking at both the timeliness and appropriateness of recognition materials offers insights into ways to improve the quality of saying "thank you" to your donors.

Any evaluation that you do is best if it includes both quantitative and qualitative data. Improved performance in your fundraising efforts should be measured both by increased quantity and better quality in order to have a well-balanced and successful program.

As these data are being collected, teams often get bogged down in comparing past and present, particularly with statistics. To avoid this pitfall, remember that your primary reason for evaluation is to make good choices about future fundraising efforts. As your evaluation plan is being developed, the leadership group should stay conscious of collecting and analyzing data that are most likely to help you be more effective in the future. Your goal: Comparing these data with past performance to discover trends to guide fundraising decisions on fundraising efforts in the future.

Several team members should gather data throughout the year. Staff or a board member with primary responsibilities for fundraising, such as a development director or board fundraising chair, will manage the collection process and provide reports to the leadership group. Whoever is collecting data should get sufficient training to understand what to look for and how to record it. When the fundraising plan is finalized and measurement criteria are developed, the leadership group member who is managing the data collection process should bring together all interested team members and spend a few hours describing what data will be collected, where to find it, and how to record it.

Frequency of Evaluation

Whoever is responsible for data collection will also need to think carefully about how often the information needs to be gathered, and how frequently it needs to be analyzed. The leadership group will need to weigh the time it takes to gather and analyze data with the time it takes to do the other management functions of organizing, planning, and implementing.

There may be some data that need to be gathered monthly, such as the number of donations received. Other data could be gathered quarterly, whereas some data will only be gathered when a solicitation has been conducted. Your team data collectors will need to know what data are being gathered and, for each piece, the frequency of the data collection.

Although the frequency of data gathering will vary, the fundraising analysis by the leadership group should be done on a regular basis. We recommend that the leadership group hold evaluation meetings at least quarterly.

To prepare for such a meeting, the person or persons responsible for data collection will need to compile the relevant information. This material should then be distributed to the leadership group well in advance of the meeting date in order to give everyone an opportunity to read and reflect on it.

Reporting too much information can overwhelm even the hardiest of souls. Therefore, keep the focus on the key data. For example, comparing and contrasting response rates from different zip codes may be crucial for an expert's analysis of a direct mail campaign, but would be a tedious and unnecessary detail to ask the leadership group to wade through. Reviewing this year's direct mail results to date versus last year's at this time, however, might produce good discussion on what is different (either positively or negatively) and generate some course corrections if needed.

Establishing the Baseline

The previous year's data is one example of a baseline that is commonly used for analyzing progress. However, there may be other baselines that seem more appropriate. On occasion, establishing a baseline may not be the right thing to do.

For example, I work with groups that decide for whatever reason to change radically the strategy they are using with a particular fundraising technique (such as direct mail). Comparing the number of pieces mailed at the end of the current year with the previous year's number of pieces might be like comparing apples to oranges.

The best rule to follow with establishing a baseline is to think about how it will help you understand what is happening currently in the organization so you can make good decisions about the future.

Reporting Progress to the Team

It is vitally important to let the whole organizational team know how well everyone is doing in fundraising. The good, the bad, and the ugly all need to be shared so the team can respond with suggestions on areas needing improvement.

The leadership group should not make any judgments about team performance without first discussing data findings with team members. There may be very important information that is not readily apparent from the data that needs to be voiced by the team. For instance, let's say that your major donor campaign was not successful in meeting the second quarter benchmark objective. It's possible to jump to the immediate conclusion that team members were not performing well in this area. However, by talking to those team members working on the major donor campaign, you might find several reasons the objective was not met. These could be internal reasons, such as a lack of necessary resources, or external reasons, such as a major fire in the community that drew the organization's focus temporarily to a different cause. Remember to find out what's going on from the source before reaching conclusions or making changes to your fundraising strategy.

Remember also to celebrate successes. Recognize team members for meeting objectives, having an impact on organizational growth, and working as a team. Success tends to generate more success if everyone feels eager and highly motivated to keep working on reaching the goals. The celebrations may tend to soften the disappointment of not being 100 percent successful.

Your evaluation process needs to include frequent report-backs from the leadership group to all team members. You may decide to meet and discuss findings with the team each time you review data. If you are using task forces for your cultivation and solicitation activities, you may also want to include task force leaders in the data review, even if they are not in the leadership group.

Evaluating the Health of Your Team

In addition to gathering and analyzing data on your team's fundraising productivity, you should also consider ways to evaluate how well the team is doing as a group. There are a couple of important reasons for taking this step.

First, it may be possible to meet your organization's annual goals and objectives in terms of dollars raised or new donors acquired without making much progress in building a strong team. I hope that you see by now that the fundraising management strategy of an organizational team is just as important as meeting annual fundraising goals.

Or you might be building a strong team but not necessarily meeting your fundraising benchmarks for the year. Remember that a team approach allows you to work smarter and to make fundraising more fun. But if you do not have prospects to cultivate, programs that are needed by your community, or a positive reputation as a nonprofit, then a fundraising team (no matter how strong they are) will not help you raise more money. This is why I recommend an internal-external analysis as one of the first steps in developing a fundraising plan.

Assuming you have the necessary fundraising elements—prospects, needed programs, and positive image—you will want to build a strong fundraising team and carefully watch over its good health. To do this, you will need a process in place to gather useful information about how the individual team members feel about their experience on the team, their relationships with each other, and the work they are doing.

As an organizational consultant, I am often contacted by nonprofit agencies that are experiencing conflict among individuals who should be working together cohesively. Common situations involve friction between boards and executive directors, or between executive directors and their staffs. The genesis of such conflict can often be traced to either (1) an unclear understanding of specific responsibilities and duties, or (2) a breakdown of communications, and sometimes both.

Teams break down and fall apart for the same reasons. Conducting a routine review of the fundraising team—by the team members—is essential to keeping everyone together and functioning smoothly.

In essence, I am suggesting a self-study that may be conducted in one of two ways, or perhaps both if the team is so inclined. First, the team may hold a written evaluation. The team members can agree to complete a questionnaire, answering an agreed-upon set of questions. Remember, these questions should be designed to reveal how the team members feel about the team, their work with each other, and the work product itself. Worksheet 12.1 is a sample form that gives some suggested questions.

WORKSHEET 12.1

Team Self-Evaluation Form

	Weak			Strong	
1. I understand and believe in the mandate of our fundraising team. Comment:	1	2	3	4	5
2. I believe in our fundraising vision and am committed to achieving it. Comment:	1	2	3	4	5
3. I believe team members are aiming for the same goals. Comment:	1	2	3	4	5
4. I feel the team conducts its activities productively. Comment:	1	2	3	4	5
5. I believe team members, including myself, know our roles on the team. Comment:	1	2	3	4	5
6. I think I communicate well with team members. Comment:	1	2	3	4	5
7. I think team meetings are timely and productive. Comment:	1	2	3	4	5
8. I can easily communicate with the leadership group and work well with their leadership. Comment:	1	2	3	4	5
9. I feel the leadership group keeps us well-informed of our progress. Comment:	1	2	3	4	5
10. I trust the team members and feel they are trusting of me. Comment:	1	2	3	4	5
11. I feel I am able to share both problems and successes with team members. Comment:	1	2	3	4	5
12. I enjoy working on this team and find it satisfying. Comment:	1	2	3	4	5

Source: *Adapted from Rees, F.,* Teamwork from Start to Finish. *San Francisco: Jossey-Bass, 1997. Reprinted with permission of the publisher.*

I caution you to work with team members to adopt your own form, using Worksheet 12.1 only as an example. There will undoubtedly be questions your team members will want to ask each other that are unique to your organization.

Some organizations will ask respondents to circle the response that best reflects how they feel. For example, *very satisfied, satisfied,* or *unsatisfied.* They also may offer team members an opportunity to add a narrative description of their response. Alternatively, questionnaires can be designed to require exclusively narrative responses.

Once completed, these questionnaires can form the basis for an insightful meeting of the leadership group. What is working and what is not working can be discussed and a summary prepared for the whole team to review and discuss further.

The second self-study option is for the team to forego the questionnaire and go directly into a full-team meeting, which may or may not be facilitated, depending on the size, preferences, and resources of the group.

The purpose of such a meeting among the team members is to assess how individuals feel about what they are doing, discover areas where things could run better, and correct small problems or misperceptions before they grow even larger.

Regardless of which evaluation process you use, a team health review should be done quarterly. This ensures that issues that may arise are quickly resolved. Quarterly reviews also help the team see their progress. If, for instance, you have several conflicts that occur during the first quarter of implementation of the model and those conflicts are no longer there by the end of the second quarter, that is progress.

Remember that building a strong team is not an overnight process. As individuals begin to work together in new and exciting ways, you may feel that progress is slow and even frustrating at times. Patience is important.

What I have witnessed in working with nonprofits that adopt a team approach to fundraising is that team-building progress is often slow the first one to two years—but there *is* progress. Usually, fundraising activities stay consistent with previous years' during this time. Then momentum builds as the team forms stronger and stronger bonds and fundraising activities increase.

Much of the success of building a team is dependent on the leadership group. It is the wisdom, patience, commitment, planning skills, and good humor of this small group that brings a team together and holds them there. If you set the stage smartly with a good leadership group, your chances for forming a strong, healthy team are huge.

Conclusion

HAVING READ THIS BOOK, I hope that you are as convinced as I am that raising funds to meet your agency's needs is not a daunting task if a team approach is adopted.

I know from personal experience that fundraising is challenging, hard work. Even more so when only one person, such as a "savior" development director or an already-overworked executive director, is doing the job. Nor should fundraising be the exclusive domain of the board of directors. Although fundraising is an important responsibility, it is not their only responsibility. To ensure agency stability and longevity, boards must also govern by setting the vision and providing oversight. The traditional strategies for conducting fundraising no longer work, if they ever did. Instead, team-based fundraising is the present and the future of successful fundraising.

As demonstrated throughout the book, the primary benefit of adopting a team-based approach is that it enables a nonprofit agency to use all its human resources. This means involving everyone connected to the nonprofit in its fundraising activities—board members, the executive director, the development director (if your nonprofit has one), staff members, and nonboard volunteers. A committed group of people, all working together to achieve common goals, can accomplish so much more than any one individual. The whole of a team is much bigger than the sum of its parts.

In the first section, I showed how to introduce and create a team-based fundraising culture in your nonprofit organization. Initiating an organizationwide discussion of the concept is the first step in the process, and it is frequently the greatest leap a nonprofit will take. Getting people comfortable with a new idea takes time and patience. But as more nonprofits adopt a team strategy and as their successes with fundraising become known, introducing this approach will become easier and easier. Until then, be patient and gently persistent.

With everyone's agreement to use a team approach to fundraising, it is time to put the team together and get to work. Each of the steps of forming, organizing, and taking action are essential to your success in fundraising. There needs to be a strong leadership group because without one, the team is likely to flounder. With this essential element of the team working together, the rest of the team is formed with clear descriptions of how the board, staff, and nonboard volunteers work together. Essential to working together is understanding where the team is headed. Your fundraising vision, mandate, and plan serve to guide and inspire every team member.

Ever mindful of the idea that fundraising should also be fun, I encourage your leadership group to add social activities to the process of forming a team approach to fundraising. Developing social bonds helps everyone work together more productively and with more support for one another. In effect, I adhere to the "work hard, play hard" adage. When you are asking people to participate in the challenging, and sometimes difficult, work of raising money, you must provide opportunities for fun and fellowship.

Your team is ready for action when your plan is set and tasks are accepted by team members. Taking action is done in several ways. All team members participate where they are most comfortable and most skilled. You will have team members who are prospect identifiers, cultivators, askers, or thankers. All are essential to fundraising, and no one should feel they have a less important job than their fellow team members.

Finally, here at the end of the book I go back to the beginning pages that introduced the concept of *teamwork.* Remember that forming your fundraising team is not the end result for you. The team's productivity, the ability to work together, and the ultimate goal of doing more great work for your community is the result you seek. A team approach to fundraising will move your organization toward fulfilling your mission in a faster, more productive way while also being fun. I am confident that you, too, will be a believer once you see the success that adopting a team-based fundraising management strategy brings to your agency. I wish you great success as you travel along through the steps in this book.

Bibliography

Allison, M., and Kaye, J. *Strategic Planning for Nonprofit Organizations: A Practical Guide and Workbook.* New York: Wiley, 1997.

Barry, B. *Strategic Planning Workbook for Nonprofit Organizations.* Boulder, Colo.: Amherst H. Wilder Foundation, 1997.

Bennis, W., and Goldsmith, J. *Learning to Lead.* Reading Mass.: Addison-Wesley, 1994.

Carver, J. *Boards that Make a Difference.* San Francisco: Jossey-Bass, 1997.

Herman, R. D., and Heimovics, R. D. *Executive Leadership in Nonprofit Organizations.* San Francisco: Jossey-Bass, 1992.

Holland, T. P. *How to Build a More Effective Board.* Washington, DC: National Center For Nonprofit Boards, 1998.

Houle, C. O. *Governing Boards.* San Francisco: Jossey-Bass, 1997.

Katzenbach, J. R., and Smith, D. K. *The Wisdom of Teams.* HarperCollins, 1993.

Joyaux, S. P. *Strategic Fund Development.* Aspen Publishers, 1971.

Mohrman, S. A., Cohen, S. G., and Mohrman, A. M., Jr. *Designing Team-Based Organizations.* San Francisco: Jossey-Bass, 1995.

Nanus, B. *Visionary Leadership: Creating a Compelling Sense of Direction for Your Organization.* San Francisco: Jossey-Bass, 1992.

Parker, G. M. *Team Players and Teamwork.* San Francisco: Jossey-Bass, 1990.

Quick, T. *Successful Team Building.* New York: AMACOM, 1992.

Rees, F. *Teamwork from Start to Finish.* San Francisco: Jossey-Bass, 1997.

Rosso, H. A., and Associates. *Achieving Excellence in Fundraising.* San Francisco: Jossey-Bass, 1991.

Index

Solicitation skills, 32–33. *See also* Donor solicitations

Staff: donor cultivation tasks of, 84; identification of potential donors by, 67; responsibilities of, 27–28, 30*t*; stewarding donor relationship by, 97

Stewarding donor relationship: case study example of, 99–100; described, 97; functions supporting, 98–99; fundraising team role in, 97–98; information gathering and, 99. *See also* Donors

Strategic Planning for Nonprofit Organizations (Kaye and Allison), 49

Strategic Planning Workbook (Barry), 49

Surveys: evaluating team health, 110–111; evaluation data from, 106; team training, 60

T

Team approach: agreement on using, 9–10, 15–16, 112–113; challenges for your organization of, 14–15; example of agreement to, 15; value of, 10–11, 112–113; worksheet for agreement to, 17. *See also* Fundraising teams

Team central, 18. *See also* Leadership group

Team development theory, 7

Team Fundraising Skills Survey worksheet, 32–33

Team orientation, 57–59

Team Self-Evaluation Form, 110

Team-oriented evaluation process, 103–105. *See also* Evaluation

Teams: advantages of using, 8; described, 6; factors for successful, 7–8. *See also* Fundraising teams

Teamwork from Start to Finish (Rees), 22

Thankathons, 95–96

Trust building, 44–45

V

Vision, 37

Vision Development worksheet, 40

Vision statement: creating a, 39–40; described, 38–39

Visionary leader, 20, 21

Visionary Leadership (Nanus), 38

W

Worksheets: Agreeing on a Team Approach, 17; Defining the Team's Mandate, 43; Developing a Cultivation Strategy, 80; Donor Identification, 69; Fund Development Analysis, 51; Leadership Characteristics, 21; Leadership Skills, 24; Major Donor Acknowledgments, 93; Setting Fundraising Goals and Objectives, 53; Team Fundraising Skills Survey, 32–33; Team Self-Evaluation Form, 110; Vision Development, 40

Written donor acknowledgments, 94–95

Y

Year-round training, 59–61